# 303

# CRUSHING
# CHESS
# TACTICS

## EASY TO HARD TACTICAL CHALLENGES!

T0154971

## ABOUT THE AUTHORS

### FRED WILSON

Fred Wilson is among the finest chess teachers and authors. Wilson has authored *303 Tricky Chess Tactics*, *303 Tricky Chess Puzzles*, and *303 Tricky Checkmates* with Bruce Alberston for Cardoza Publishing. He is the owner of Fred Wilson Chess Books in New York City.

### BRUCE ALBERSTON

Bruce Alberston, a well-known chess trainer and teacher in the New York city area, collaborated with Fred Wilson on *202 Surprising Mates*, *303 Tricky Chess Tactics*, *303 Tricky Chess Puzzles*, and *303 Tricky Checkmates* with Wilson. He is also the sole author of two books: *51 Chess Openings* and *Savage Chess Opening Traps*. Alberston did significant research and analysis for Bruce Pandolfini (who has written 17 books for Simon & Shuster).

# FRED WILSON & BRUCE ALBERSTON

# 303

# CRUSHING CHESS TACTICS

## EASY TO HARD TACTICAL CHALLENGES!

---

## CARDOZA PUBLISHING

Copyright © 2018 by Fred Wilson & Bruce Alberston
- All Rights Reserved -

Formerly titled *303 More Tricky Chess Puzzles*

Library of Congress Catalog Card No: 2017955772
ISBN: 978-1-58042-361-8

Visit our web site—www.cardozabooks.com—or write
for a full list of books and computer strategies.

## CARDOZA PUBLISHING

P.O. Box 98115, Las Vegas, NV 89193
Phone (800) 577-WINS
email: cardozabooks@aol.com

# TABLE OF CONTENTS

# SYMBOLS AND ABBREVIATIONS

**K** stands for King
**Q** stands for Queen
**R** stands for Rook
**B** stands for Bishop
**N** stands for Knight
**There** is no symbol for the pawn. A pawn move is indicated by a lowercase letter which identifies the file of the moving pawn. (e4 shows that a pawn has moved to the e4 square. If a capital letter had preceded the letter, such as Ne4, it would shows a piece had moved there, in this case, the Knight.)

---

**x** stands for a capture
**0-0** stands for King-side castling
**0-0-0** stands for Queen-side castling

---

**...** the three dots following a move number indicate a Black move. (2...e6 indicates that Black's second move was to bring the pawn to e6.)
**/** with a capital letter immediately to the right of the slash mark indicates that a pawn is promoted to a piece. (h1/Q shows that the pawn on the h file moved to the h1 square – thus a Black pawn – and was promoted to a Queen.)

---

**+** stands for check
**#** stands for checkmate

---

**!** means very good move
**!!** means brilliant move
**?** means bad move
**??** means losing blunder

# INTRODUCTION

*Tactics are tricks that win stuff!*
—A ten year old chessplayer

*The essential for the student is to play over and study again and again what he has learned until it becomes part of his very self.*
—Dr. S. Tarrasch

In chess, ultimately you want to win your opponent's king. And whether you accomplish this by winning some or all of his pieces, thereby achieving overwhelming material superiority, or through a successful mating attack, the result will be the same—checkmate.

So, it is essential to master tactics if you want to get good at chess and give yourself that opportunity. But it won't necessarily be easy, you'll probably have to work at it.

If you think you're already good enough at tactics, take a quick look at the position on the next page—it is White's move—and decide what you think White should do.

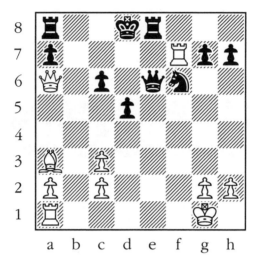

Most of our students, adults and children, want to play **1. Qb7**, seeing only that White is threatening both the a1 rook and **2. Qc7#**, often commenting that even after **1...Rc8**, to prevent mate, that Black's position is "a mess." They completely overlook Black's tactical possibilities; that after **1...Qe3+** White must submit to a draw by **2. Kf1 Qf4+; 3. Kg1 Qe3+**, with perpetual check, as **2. Kh1??** would allow Black to win with **2...Qe1+!**, and mate next move!

Surprisingly few players spot the correct answer quickly, namely that **1. Qa5+!** (sometimes you have to move "backwards" to go forwards!) **Kc8; 2. Qc7#** is a forced mate in two.

However, even if you didn't solve this fast it doesn't necessarily mean you need to work on your tactics. Or does it? Consider the following position, with White to move, and ask yourself if **1. e4**, forking two minor pieces, is a good, bad or mediocre move?

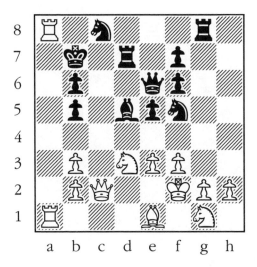

Answer: it is way worse than mediocre! After **1. e4??** Black sets up a fork of his own by **2...Rxg2+!** either skewering the White king and queen after **2. Kf1 Rxc2**, or winning White's queen with a fork by **2. Kxg2 Nxe3+**.

But, wait a minute, what should White have played? Well, if you can calculate and visualize four moves deep, and your attacking instincts were properly honed by a lot of solving practice, you would have seen that after **1. Qxc8+! Rxc8; 2. R/1a7+ Kc6; 3. Rxc8+** (you had to visualize that now the c8 rook is *en prise*) **Kd6; 4. Bb4#**.

Still not convinced that you need to study tactics again and again until they become part of your very self? Then look at the position below and see if you can discover how Woman World Champion Nona Gaprindashvili, as Black, created a winning double attack against Sznapik at Sandomir, in 1976.

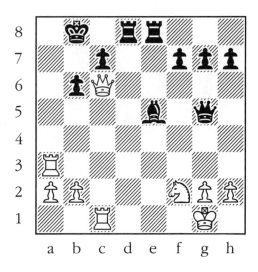

Boy, things look bad for Black, don't they? She is threatened with a seemingly unstoppable mate at a8. Well, actually Black does have everything under control if you can find **1...Qxc1+!; 2. Qxc1 Bxb2!** winning a second rook, leaving Black with a winning material superiority as **3. Qxb2??** allows **3...Re1** mate!

If you weren't able to solve all of these problems then we believe you certainly do need this book, and probably also our earlier books on chess tactics, or something like them! On Fred's internet radio chess show *Chess & Books with Fred Wilson*, on the website www.chess.fm, the well-known and popular American Grandmaster Maurice Ashley talked about how he studied and solved twenty-five middlegame positions each night before bed and how that "really helped me become an International Master."

We believe, as in our earlier books, *303 Tricky Checkmates, 303 Tricky Chess Tactics,* and *303 Tricky Chess Puzzles,* we have created another very practical tactics workbook which will help you improve your game. As usual, we use only two large, clear diagrams per page, to facilitate calculating and visualizing the possibilities (while not causing you eyestrain!). About one third of the positions are "Black to Move" to give you practice at looking at things from Black's perspective.

Parenthetical hints are provided at the top of each diagram, and in this book we have used the reinforcing technique of having two examples of the same tactic on each page. Also, we have often included written explanations with the solutions at the end to help clarify difficult variations and concepts.

Finally, we have included a tactics index to help you easily locate many examples of the same tactic. This will facilitate your working specifically on any type of tactic that you find particularly difficult. We encourage you to go through this book more than once—indeed, several times—until you become quite comfortable at solving *all* the positions.

Remember you don't have to quite emulate GM Ashley's dedication to benefit from this book. You can pick it up whenever you have a chance, work on the puzzles for five or ten minutes at a time, and then continue later. If you set your own pace in figuring out the answers we're sure you'll actually start to enjoy the challenges! And positions like the one below, with White to move, probably won't seem so baffling:

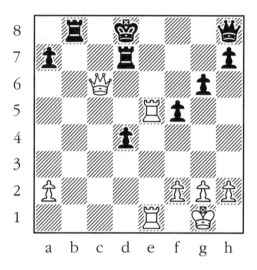

Hmm…this looks pretty hard! If White tries **1. Rd5** it looks like Black can hold on with **1…Qg7!** while **1. Re8+ Qxd8; 2. Rxe8+ Kxe8** seems to actually be a good transaction for Black with his dangerous passed d-pawn. We believe that when you think you should "have something" but can't find it, try to determine what is the one piece that's holding your opponent's position together and then see if you can eliminate it! In this case it must be the d7 rook so…do you see it now?

Yup, White has a forced win with **1. Re7!! Rbb7 (1… Rxe7; 2. Qd6+ Kc8; 3. Rc1+ Kb7; 4. Qc6#) 2.Rxd7+ Rxd7; 3. Qa8+ Kc7; 4. Qxh8**.

Hopefully, if you'll just stick with us, and start practicing solving chess puzzles whenever possible, you'll also begin to find cool combinations like this in your own games. Now, it's up to you.

Get going!

—Fred Wilson & Bruce Alberston

# SECTION 1

# EASY

The chapter heading "Easy" belies the title of the book.

Naturally, whether you find the positions of chapter one easy or not depends on your level of chess development. Still, we have to start someplace. Here at any rate, is where you develop your basic arsenal of tactical ideas.

Included in the chapter are the eleven most common tactical themes.

**En prise**, the capture of an undefended or insufficiently defended unit, forms the foundation. Because it is the simplest idea of all we tend to take it for granted. But if you observe carefully, at the conclusion of every successful tactical operation, you'll find something *en prise* at the end.

The **mating attack** of course is directed at the king. Checkmate itself is an example of the **trapping** theme. And when the opponent succeeds in warding off the mate it will invariably be at the cost of material, so it still registers as a successful attack.

Not so easy to ward off is the double attack, when two or more enemy pieces come under fire. These double or multiple threats are illustrated by the **fork, pin, skewer,** and **discovery.**

The defensive structure may itself be brought into question. In these instances the undermining mechanisms most commonly used are **removing the guard, driving off,** and **overload.**

Finally, pawn **promotion** represents a significant increase in attacking force. It usually occurs in the endgame stage and is mostly decisive.

While the vast majority of the positions are designed to gain an advantage, we must note that the defender can also resort to these same tactical devices to try and stay afloat. Numbers 8, 42, and 51 fall into this category.

## 1. *Black to Move*
(En Prise)

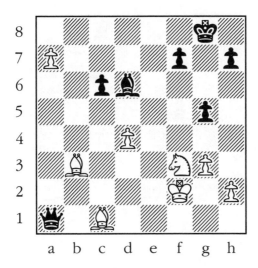

## 2. *White to Move*
(En Prise)

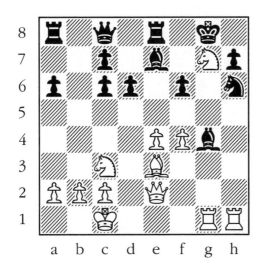

**15**

### 3. *White to Move*
(Trapping)

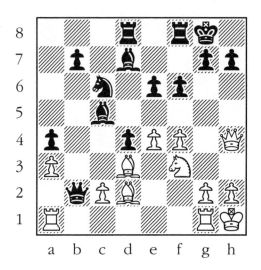

### 4. *White to Move*
(Trapping)

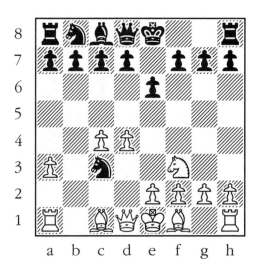

### 5. *Black to Move*
(Fork)

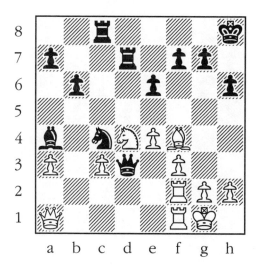

### 6. *White to Move*
(Fork)

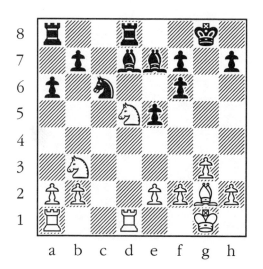

### 7. *White to Move*
(Pin)

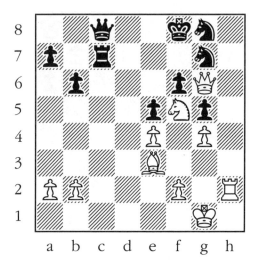

### 8. *Black to Move*
(Pin)

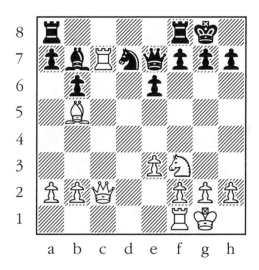

### 9. *White to Move*
(Mating Attack)

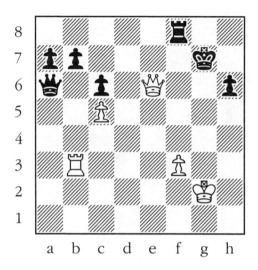

### 10. *White to Move*
(Mating Attack)

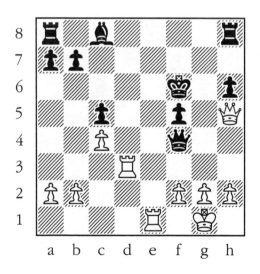

## 11. *Black to Move*
### (En Prise)

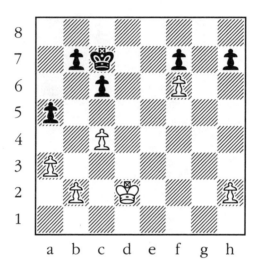

## 12. *Black to Move*
### (En Prise)

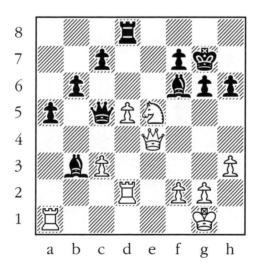

### 13. *Black to Move*
(Promotion)

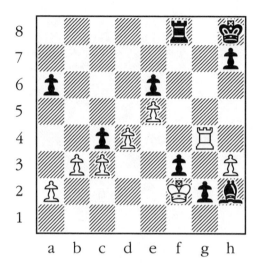

### 14. *Black to Move*
(Promotion)

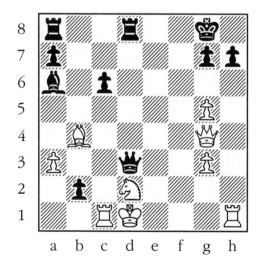

## 15. *White to Move*
(Driving Off)

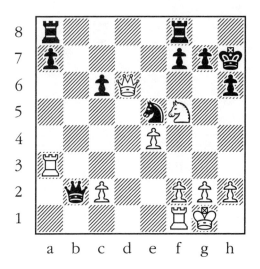

## 16. *White to Move*
(Driving Off)

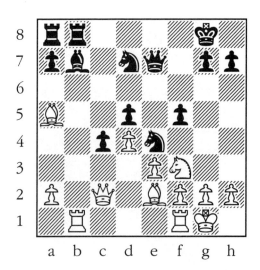

### 17. *White to Move*
(Overload)

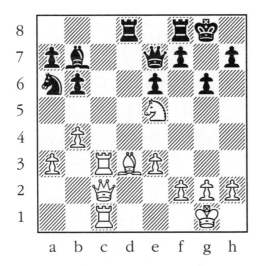

### 18. *White to Move*
(Overload)

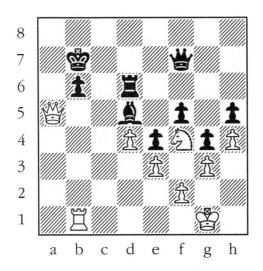

### 19. *Black to Move*
(Removing the Guard)

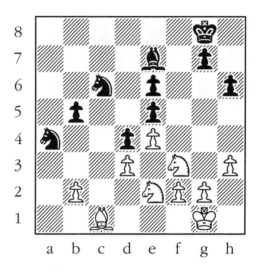

### 20. *White to Move*
(Removing the Guard)

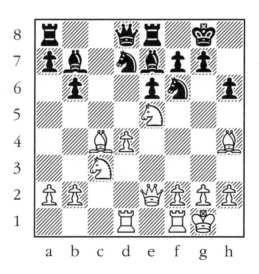

### 21. *White to Move*
(En Prise)

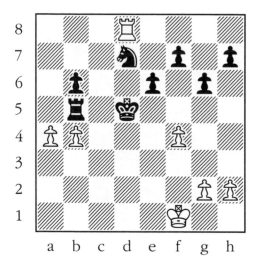

### 22. *White to Move*
(En Prise)

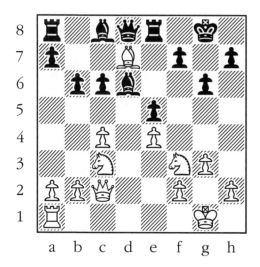

### 23. *Black to Move*
(Trapping)

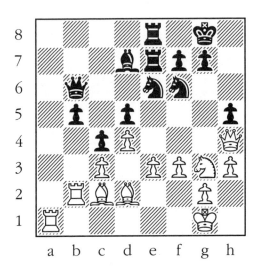

### 24. *White to Move*
(Trapping)

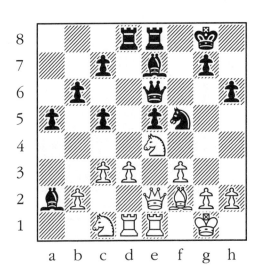

## 25. *White to Move*
### (Fork)

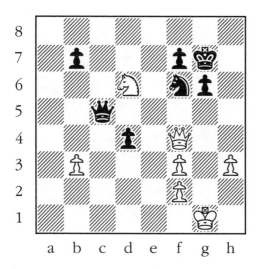

## 26. *White to Move*
### (Fork)

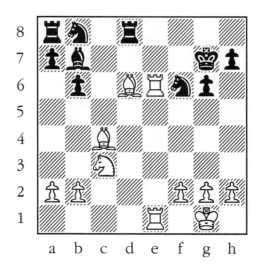

### 27. *White to Move*
(Pin)

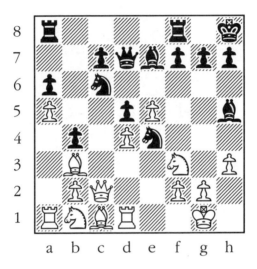

### 28. *White to Move*
(Pin)

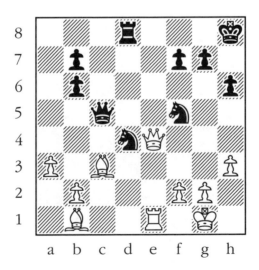

### 29. *White to Move*
(Mating Attack)

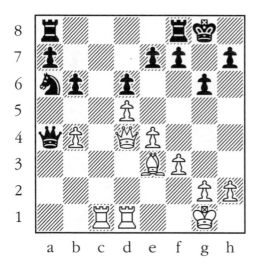

### 30. *White to Move*
(Mating Attack)

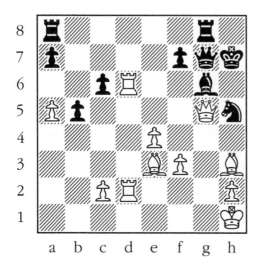

## 31. *Black to Move*
### (En Prise)

## 32. *White to Move*
### (En Prise)

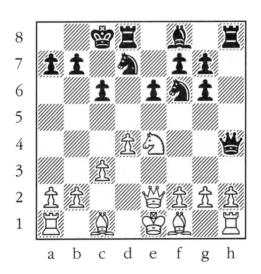

## 33. *White to Move*
(Promotion)

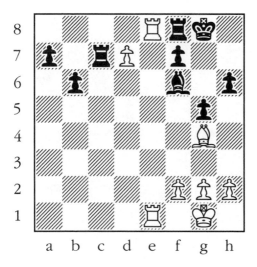

## 34. *White to Move*
(Promotion)

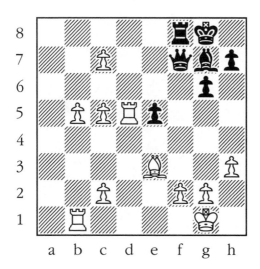

### 35. *Black to Move*
(Driving Off)

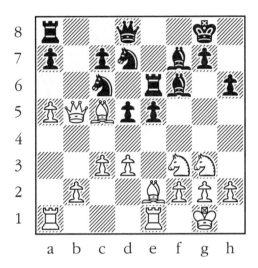

### 36. *White to Move*
(Driving Off)

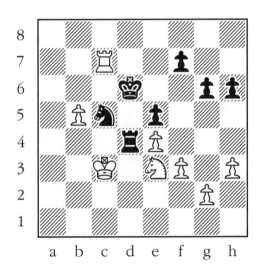

### 37. *White to Move*
(Skewer)

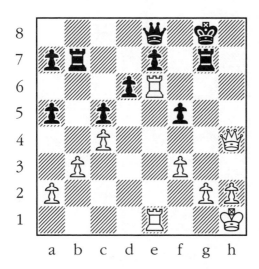

### 38. *Black to Move*
(Skewer)

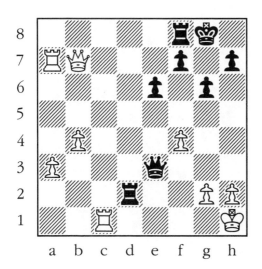

### 39. *White to Move*
(Removing the Guard)

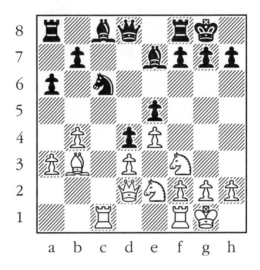

### 40. *White to Move*
(Removing the Guard)

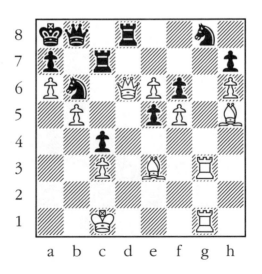

## 41. *Black to Move*
(En Prise)

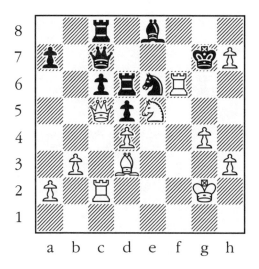

## 42. *Black to Move*
(En Prise)

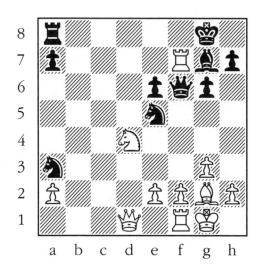

## 43. *White to Move*
(Trapping)

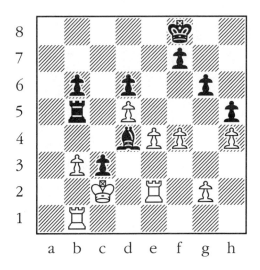

## 44. *White to Move*
(Trapping)

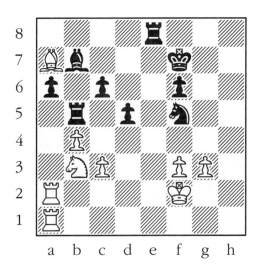

## 45. *White to Move*
(Fork)

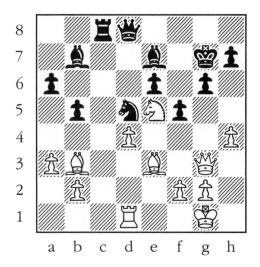

## 46. *White to Move*
(Fork)

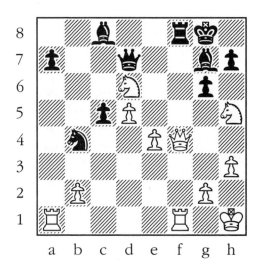

### 47. *Black to Move*
(Pin)

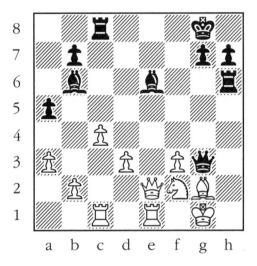

### 48. *White to Move*
(Pin)

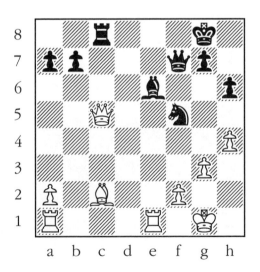

### 49. *Black to Move*
(Mating Attack)

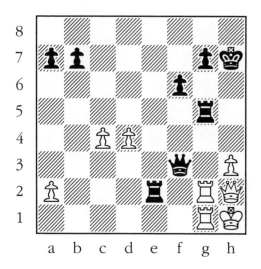

### 50. *Black to Move*
(Mating Attack)

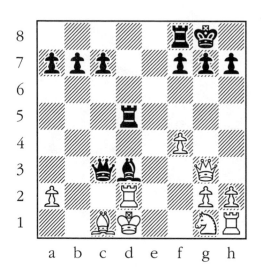

## 51. *Black to Move*
### (En Prise)

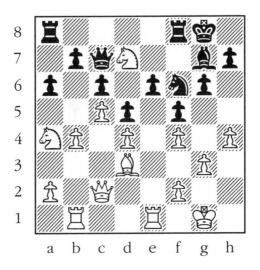

## 52. *Black to Move*
### (En Prise)

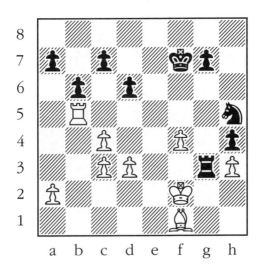

### 53. *White to Move*
(Promotion )

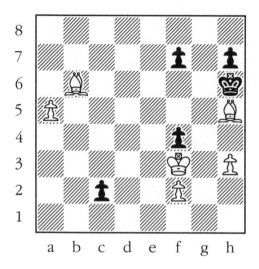

### 54. *Black to Move*
(Promotion)

## 55. *White to Move*
(Fork)

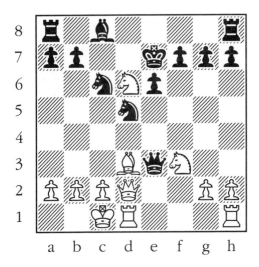

## 56. *White to Move*
(Fork)

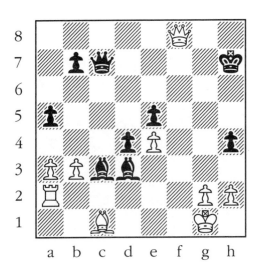

### 57. *White to Move*
(Overload)

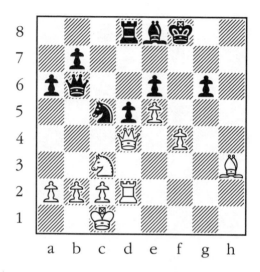

### 58. *Black to Move*
(Overload)

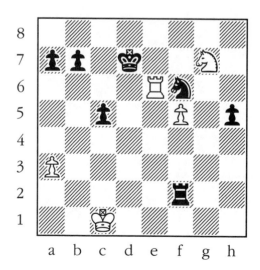

## 59. *White to Move*
(Removing the Guard)

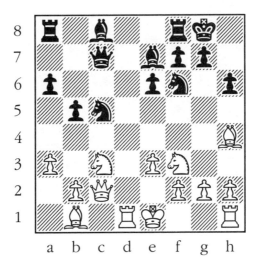

## 60. *Black to Move*
(Removing the Guard)

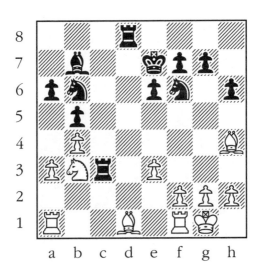

### 61. *White to Move*
(Discovery)

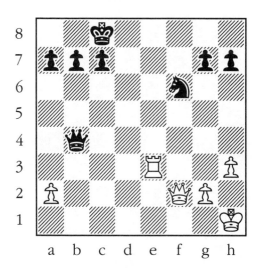

### 62. *Black to Move*
(Discovery)

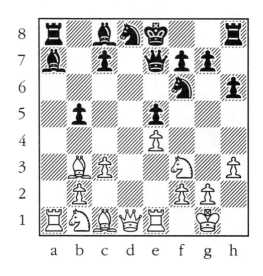

### 63. *White to Move*
(Trapping)

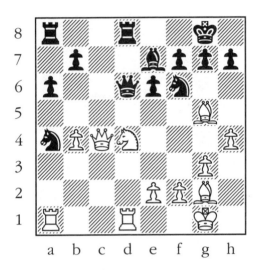

### 64. *White to Move*
(Trapping)

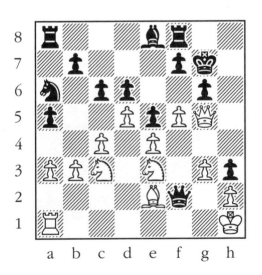

### 65. *Black to Move*
(Fork)

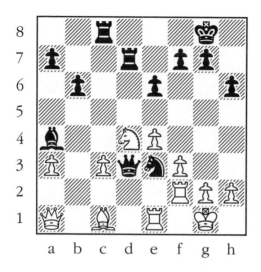

### 66. *White to Move*
(Fork)

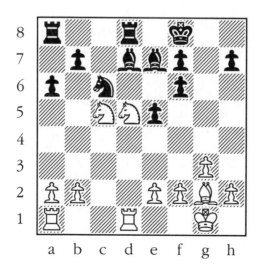

### 67. *White to Move*
(Pin)

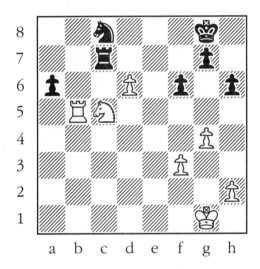

### 68. *White to Move*
(Pin)

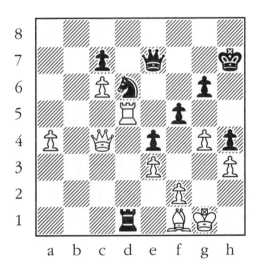

### 69. *White to Move*
(Mating Attack)

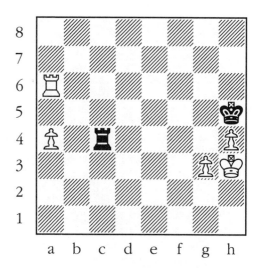

### 70. *Black to Move*
(Mating Attack)

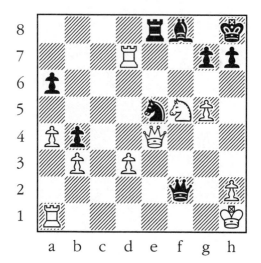

## 71. *White to Move*
(Discovery)

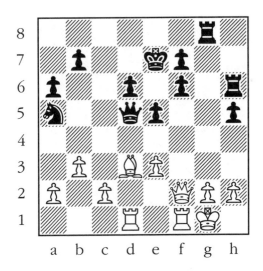

## 72. *White to Move*
(Discovery)

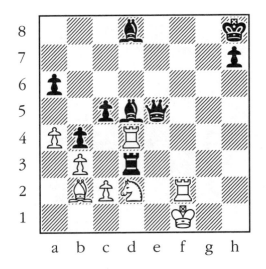

### 73. *White to Move*
(Promotion)

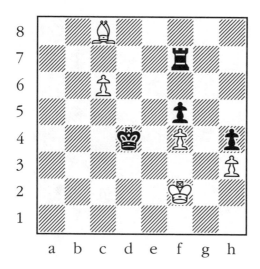

### 74. *White to Move*
(Promotion)

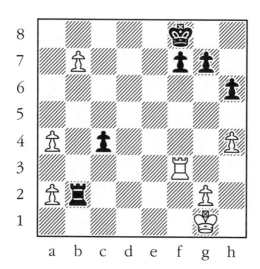

### 75. *White to Move*
(Driving Off)

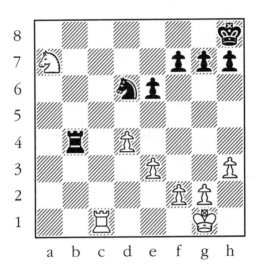

### 76. *White to Move*
(Driving Off)

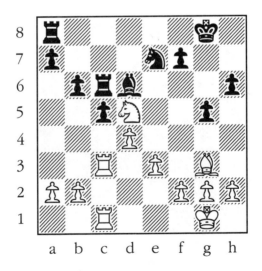

### 77. *Black to Move*
(Pin)

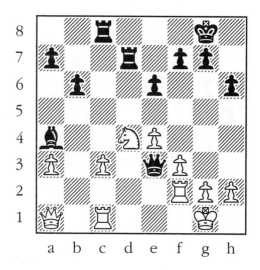

### 78. *White to Move*
(Pin)

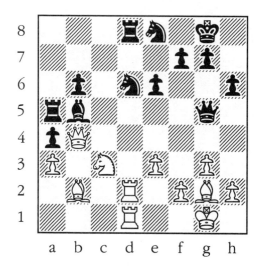

### 79. *White to Move*
(Mating Attack)

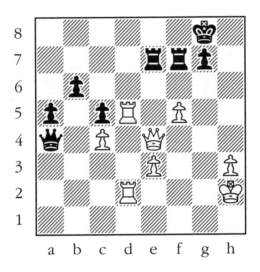

### 80. *Black to Move*
(Mating Attack)

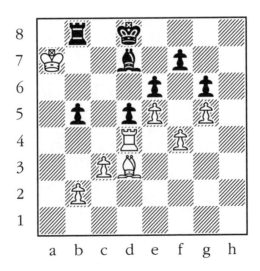

## 81. *White to Move*
(Discovery)

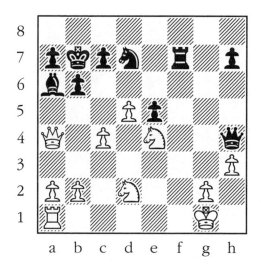

## 82. *White to Move*
(Discovery)

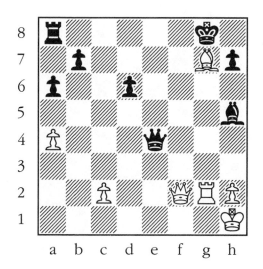

### 83. *White to Move*
(Trapping)

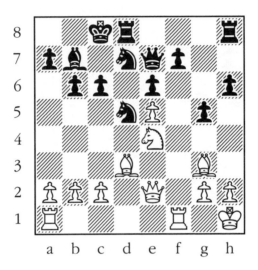

### 84. *Black to Move*
(Trapping)

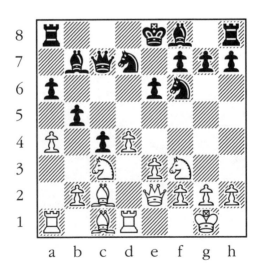

### 85. *Black to Move*
(Fork)

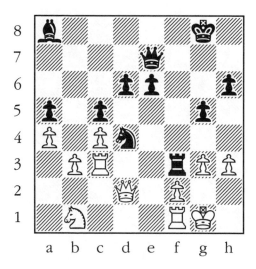

### 86. *White to Move*
(Fork)

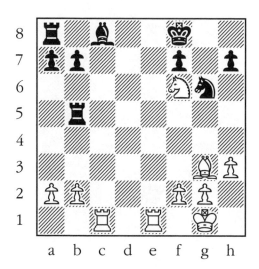

### 87. *White to Move*
(Pin)

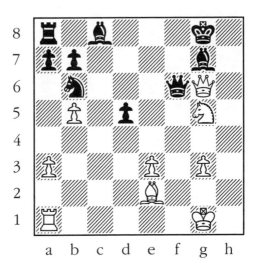

### 88. *Black to Move*
(Pin)

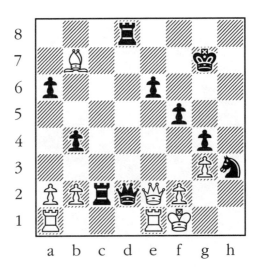

### 89. *White to Move*
(Overload)

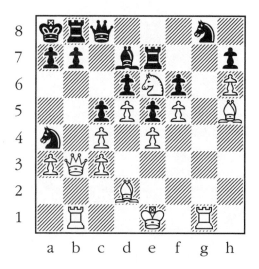

### 90. *Black to Move*
(Overload)

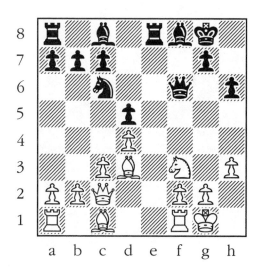

## 91. *Black to Move*
(Discovery)

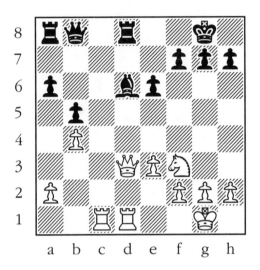

## 92. *Black to Move*
(Discovery)

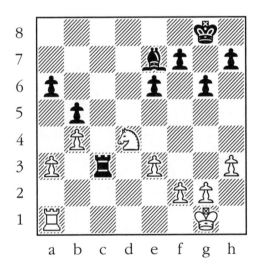

### 93. *White to Move*
(Promotion)

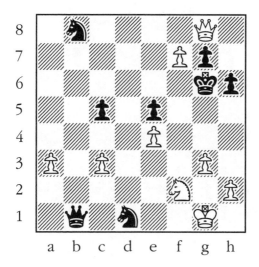

### 94. *White to Move*
(Promotion)

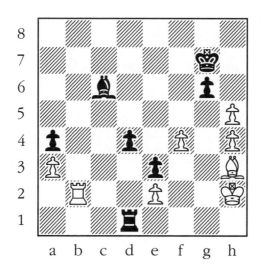

### 95. *Black to Move*
(Driving Off)

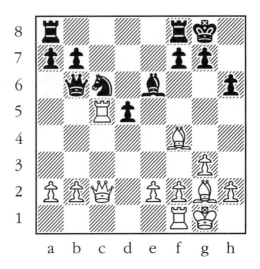

### 96. *Black to Move*
(Driving Off)

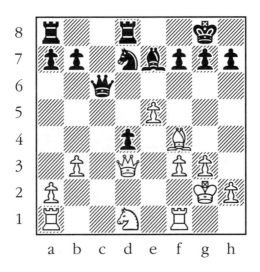

## 97. *White to Move*
(Skewer)

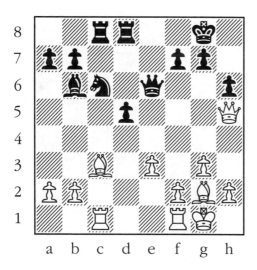

## 98. *White to Move*
(Skewer)

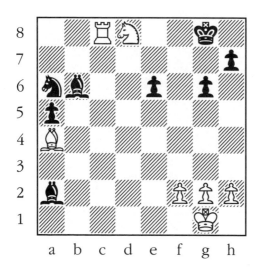

63

## 99. *Black to Move*
(Removing the Guard)

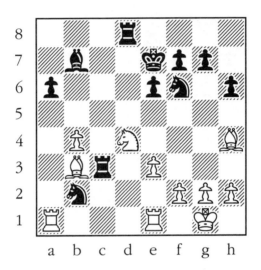

## 100. *White to Move*
(Removing the Guard)

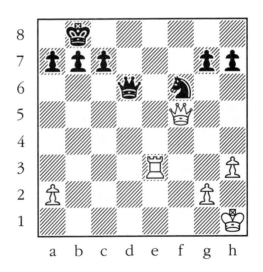

# SECTION 2

# MEDIUM

This Section is nothing more than a logical extension of Section One. We have exactly the same eleven tactical themes, only a bit more difficult to implement. This degree of difficulty applies to the chapter as a whole, not to individual problems.

If you've gone through the puzzles of the first chapter conscientiously, then you should be quite familiar with all the standard tricks. Hopefully, they should now be at your fingertips.

By now your eyes have been conditioned to spot the most forcing moves of the position: captures, checks and threats to capture or give checkmate. You generally start with one of these since they force the opponent to respond in a limited way, thus narrowing down the avenues of calculation.

Tactical technique when absorbed does not demand any great searching facilities. Rather the fundamental ideas just leap out at you. That's the technique part. You instantly focus on what looks important—those nasty captures and checks. Number 106, a fork, is a good simple example. The eye immediately spots the captures on f7 and the knight check at d6. All the player has to do is sort out which comes first.

As previously noted, we've slipped in some defensive resources, the purpose of which is to keep the position from deteriorating. Numbers 104, 166, and 167 come to mind.

Along similar lines is the preventative sacrifice, played by the attacker to nullify an enemy threat, before resuming the initiative himself. These are spectacularly illustrated in examples 131 and 154.

## 101. *White to Move*
(En Prise)

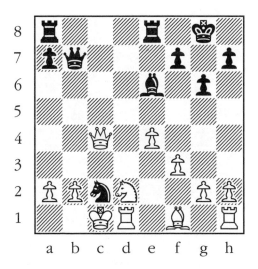

## 102. *White to Move*
(En Prise)

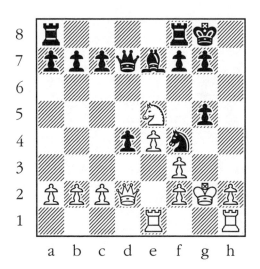

### 103. *Black to Move*
(Trapping)

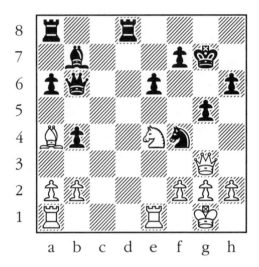

### 104. *White to Move*
(Trapping)

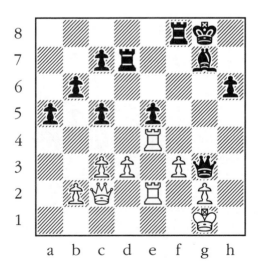

## 105. *White to Move*
(Fork)

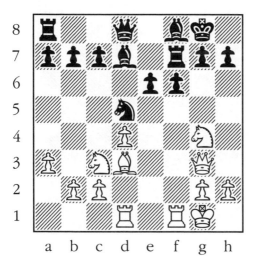

## 106. *White to Move*
(Fork)

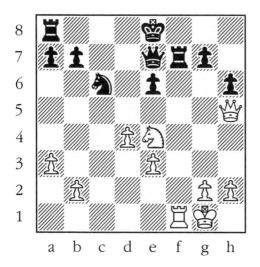

### 107. *White to Move*
(Pin)

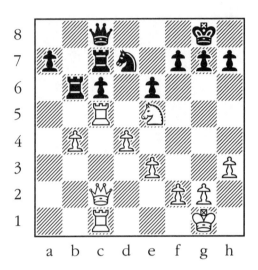

### 108. *White to Move*
(Pin)

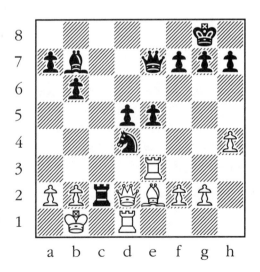

### 109. *Black to Move*
(Mating Attack)

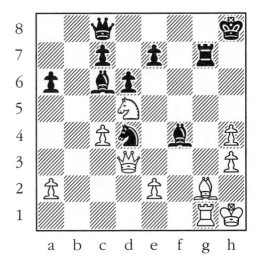

### 110. *White to Move*
(Mating Attack)

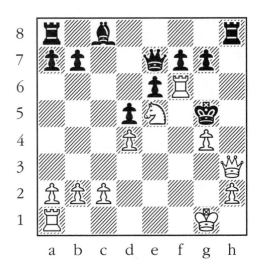

### 111. *White to Move*
(Discovery)

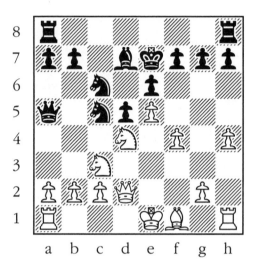

### 112. *White to Move*
(Discovery)

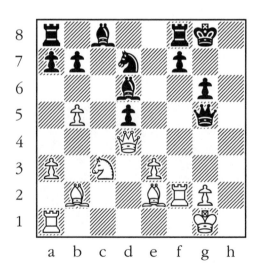

### 113. *White to Move*
(Promotion)

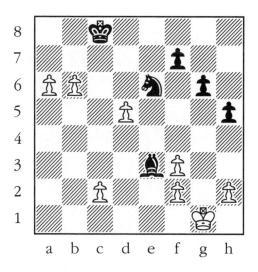

### 114. *White to Move*
(Promotion)

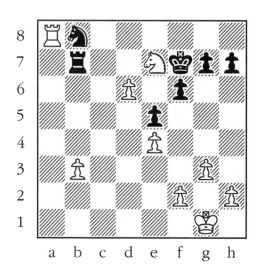

**115.** *White to Move*
(Driving Off)

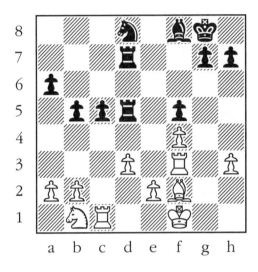

**116.** *White to Move*
(Driving Off)

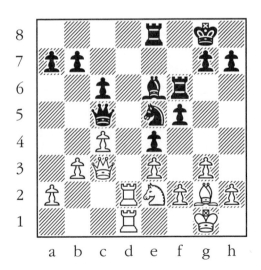

### 117. *Black to Move*
(Overload)

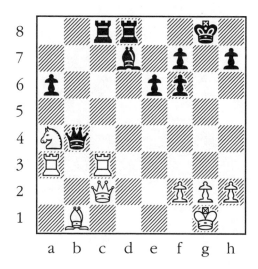

### 118. *Black to Move*
(Overload)

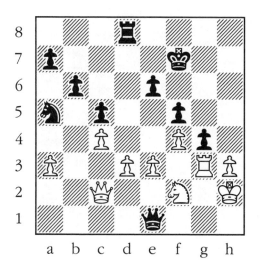

### 119. *White to Move*
(Removing the Guard)

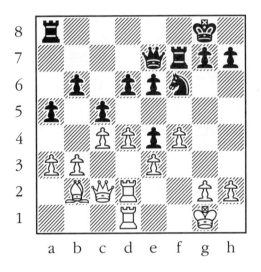

### 120. *Black to Move*
(Removing the Guard)

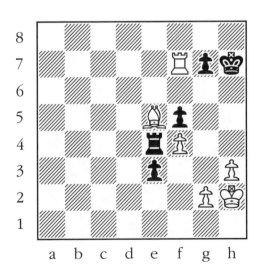

## 121. *White to Move*
(En Prise)

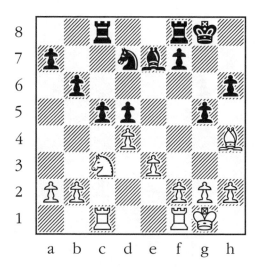

## 122. *White to Move*
(En Prise)

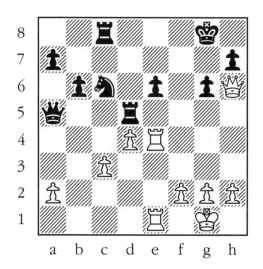

### 123. *Black to Move*
(Trapping)

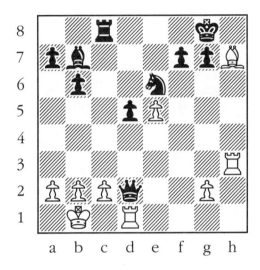

### 124. *White to Move*
(Trapping)

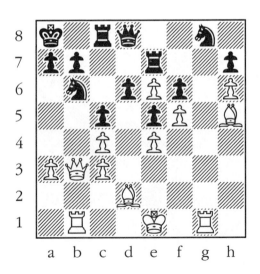

### 125. *White to Move*
(Fork)

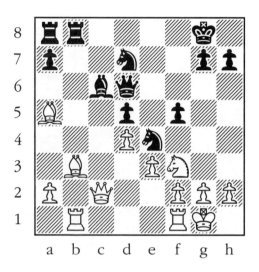

### 126. *White to Move*
(Fork)

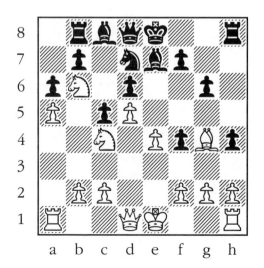

## 127. *White to Move*
### (Pin)

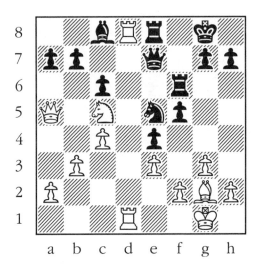

## 128. *White to Move*
### (Pin)

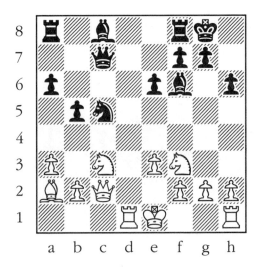

## 129. *White to Move*
(Mating Attack)

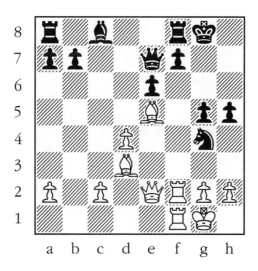

## 130. *Black to Move*
(Mating Attack)

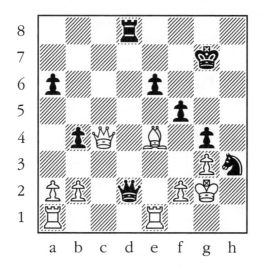

## 131. *Black to Move*
(Removing the Guard)

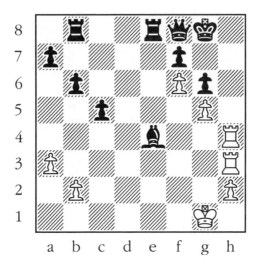

## 132. *White to Move*
(Removing the Guard)

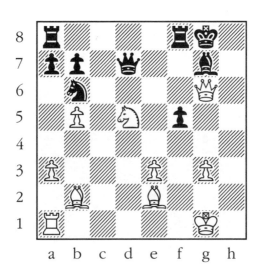

## 133. *White to Move*
(Promotion)

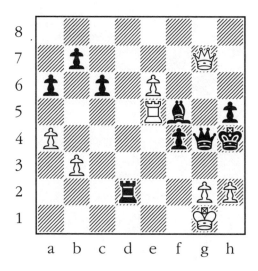

## 134. *White to Move*
(Promotion)

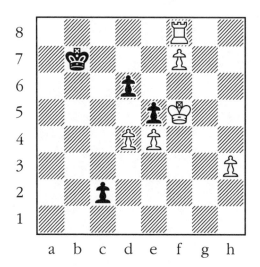

### 135. *White to Move*
(Driving Off)

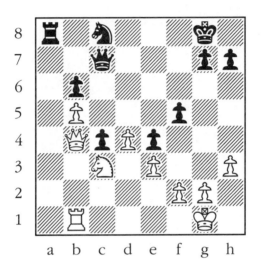

### 136. *White to Move*
(Driving Off)

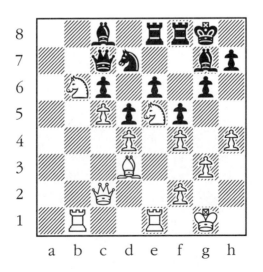

## 137. *White to Move*
(Skewer)

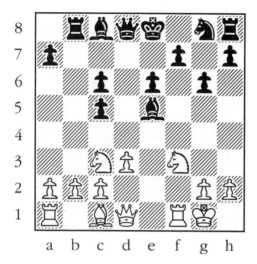

## 138. *White to Move*
(Skewer)

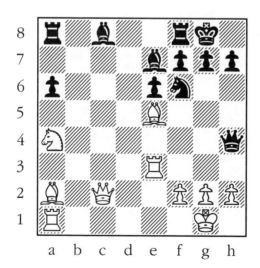

## 139. *White to Move*
(Removing the Guard)

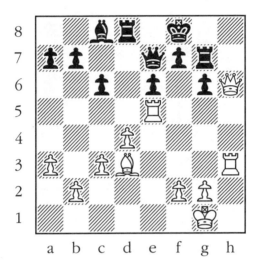

## 140. *White to Move*
(Removing the Guard)

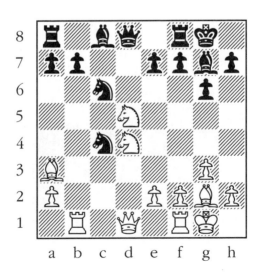

### 141. *Black to Move*
(En Prise)

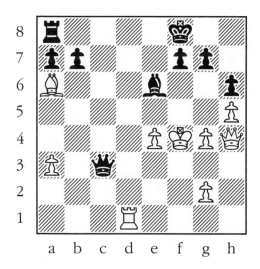

### 142. *Black to Move*
(En Prise)

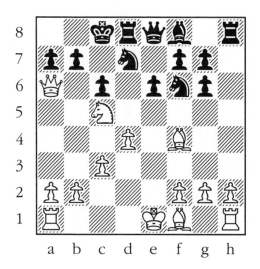

### 143. *White to Move*
(Trapping)

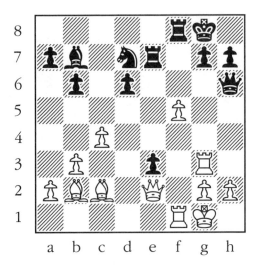

### 144. *White to Move*
(Trapping)

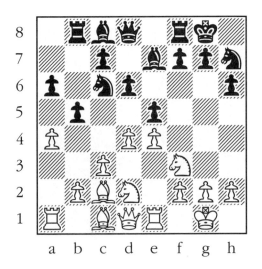

### 145. *White to Move*
(Fork)

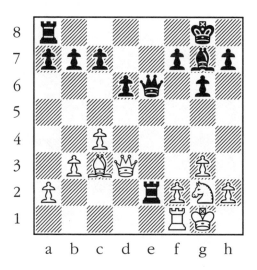

### 146. *White to Move*
(Fork)

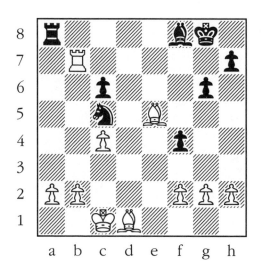

### 147. *White to Move*
(Pin)

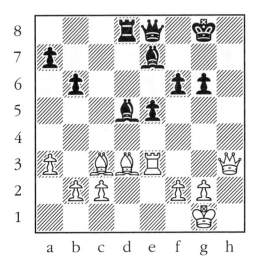

### 148. *Black to Move*
(Pin)

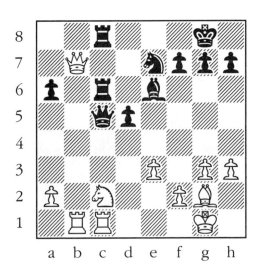

### 149. *White to Move*
(Mating Attack)

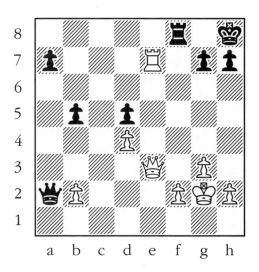

### 150. *Black to Move*
(Mating Attack)

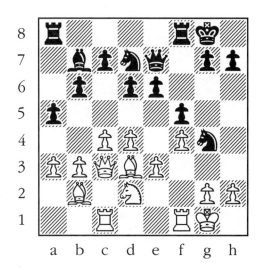

### 151. *Black to Move*
(Discovery)

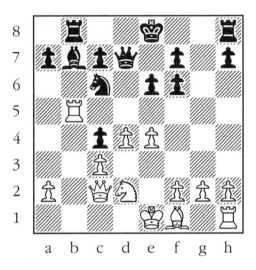

### 152. *White to Move*
(Discovery)

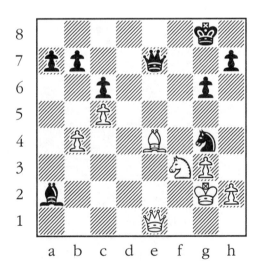

## 153. *Black to Move*
(Promotion )

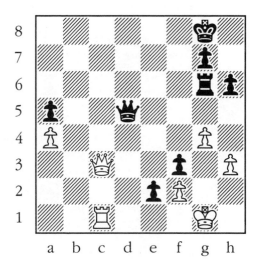

## 154. *White to Move*
(Promotion)

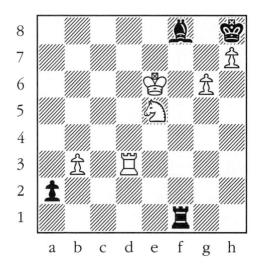

### 155. *White to Move*
(Driving Off)

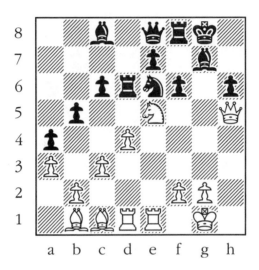

### 156. *White to Move*
(Driving Off)

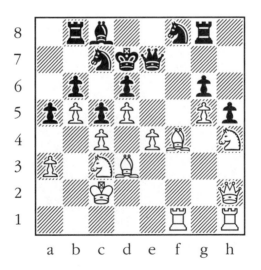

### 157. *White to Move*
(Overload)

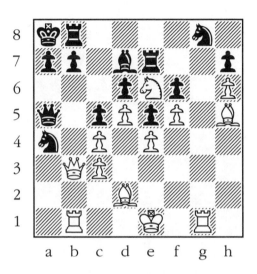

### 158. *White to Move*
(Overload)

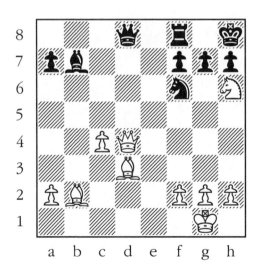

### 159. *White to Move*
(Removing the Guard)

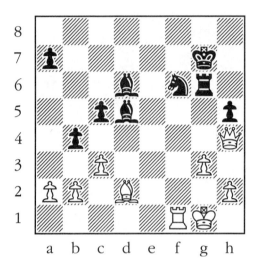

### 160. *White to Move*
(Removing the Guard)

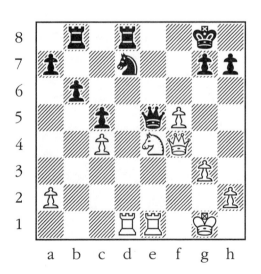

### 161. *Black to Move*
(En Prise)

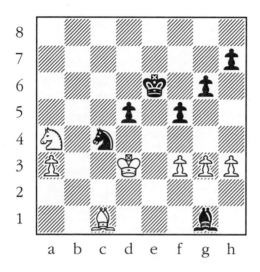

### 162. *White to Move*
(En Prise)

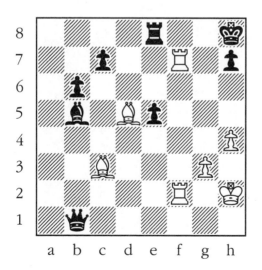

## 163. *Black to Move*
(Trapping)

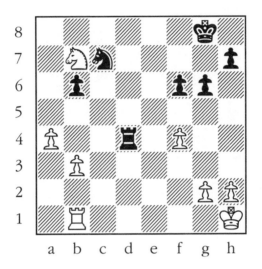

## 164. *White to Move*
(Trapping)

### 165. *White to Move*
(Fork)

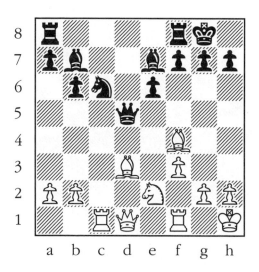

### 166. *Black to Move*
(Fork)

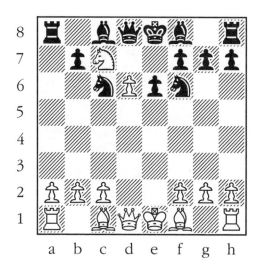

### 167. *White to Move*
(Pin)

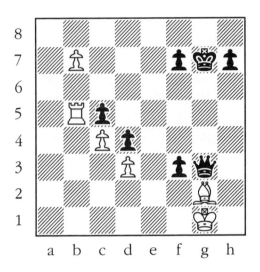

### 168. *White to Move*
(Pin)

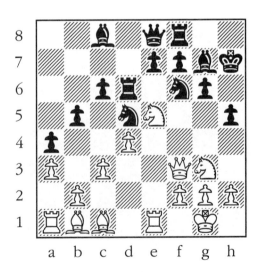

### 169. *Black to Move*
(Mating Attack)

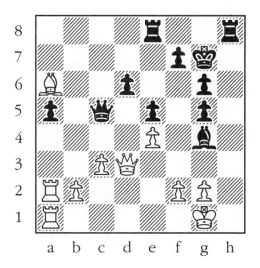

### 170. *White to Move*
(Mating Attack)

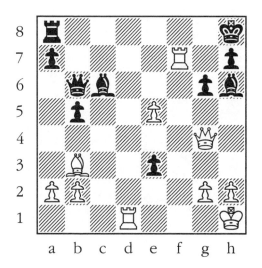

### 171. *White to Move*
(Discovery)

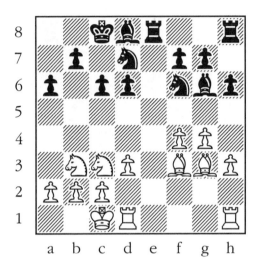

### 172. *White to Move*
(Discovery)

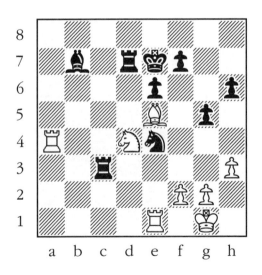

### 173. *White to Move*
(Removing the Guard)

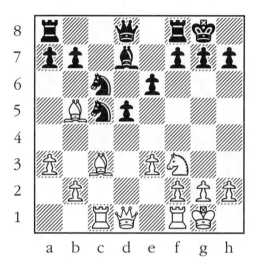

### 174. *White to Move*
(Removing the Guard)

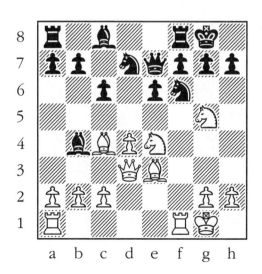

## 175. *Black to Move*
(Fork)

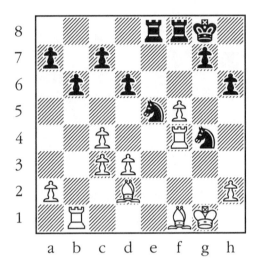

## 176. *White to Move*
(Fork)

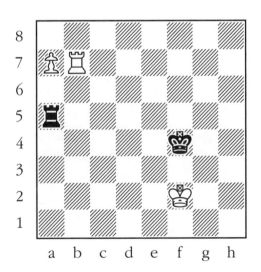

### 177. *White to Move*
(Pin)

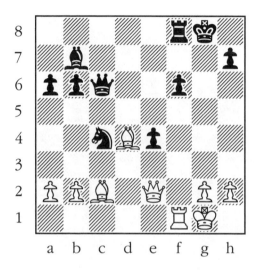

### 178. *Black to Move*
(Pin)

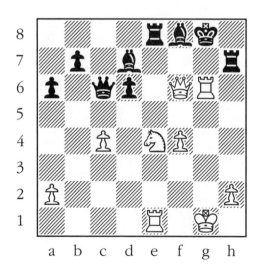

## 179. *Black to Move*
(Mating Attack)

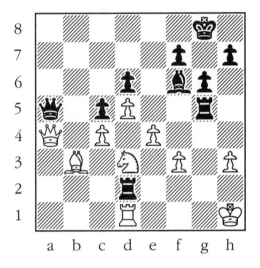

## 180. *White to Move*
(Mating Attack)

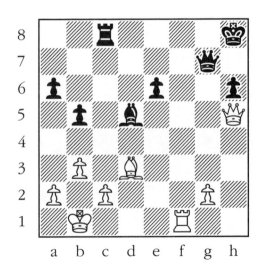

## 181. *White to Move*
(Discovery)

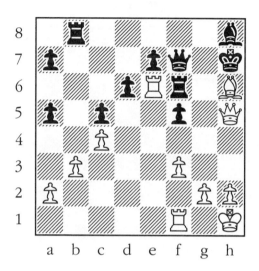

## 182. *White to Move*
(Discovery)

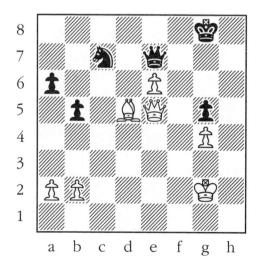

### 183. *White to Move*
(Promotion)

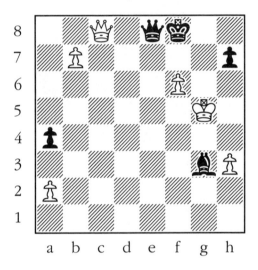

### 184. *Black to Move*
(Promotion)

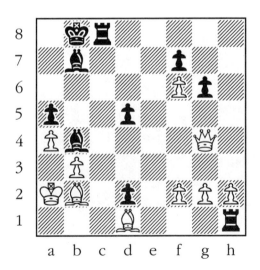

### 185. *White to Move*
(Fork)

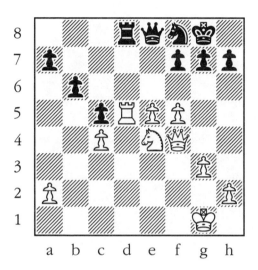

### 186. *White to Move*
(Fork)

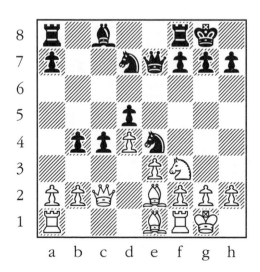

### 187. *White to Move*
(Pin)

### 188. *White to Move*
(Pin)

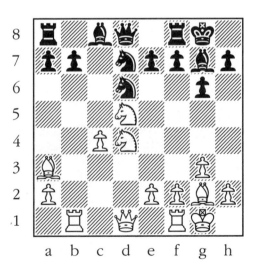

**189.** *Black to Move*
(Mating Attack)

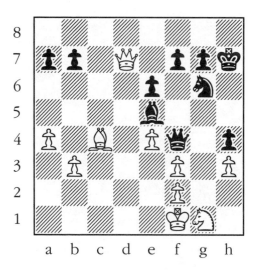

**190.** *White to Move*
(Mating Attack)

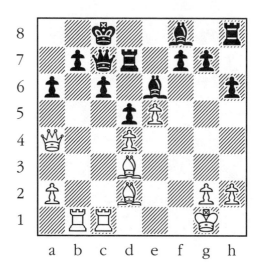

## 191. *White to Move*
(Discovery)

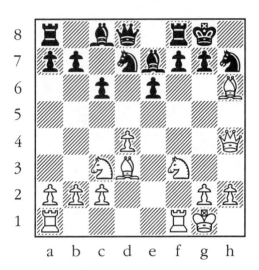

## 192. *White to Move*
(Discovery)

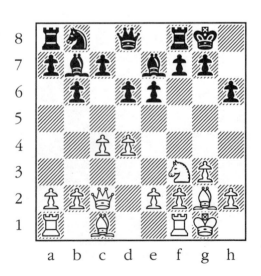

### 193. *Black to Move*
(Overload)

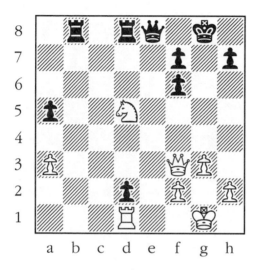

### 194. *White to Move*
(Overload)

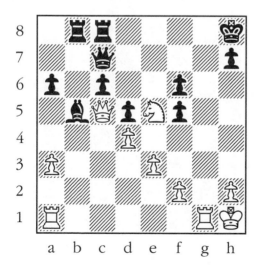

### 195. *Black to Move*
(Driving Off)

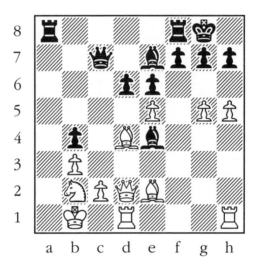

### 196. *Black to Move*
(Driving Off)

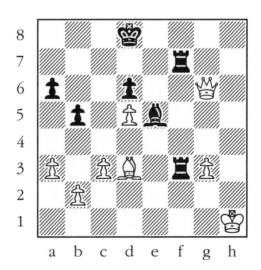

### 197. *White to Move*
(Skewer)

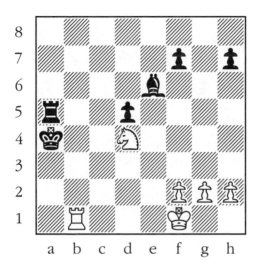

### 198. *White to Move*
(Skewer)

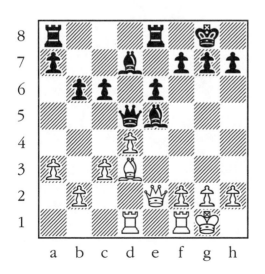

## 199. *White to Move*
(Removing the Guard)

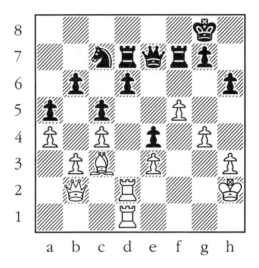

## 200. *White to Move*
(Removing the Guard)

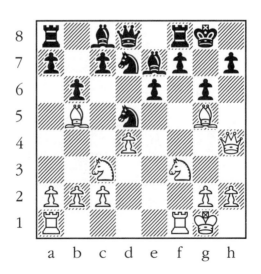

# SECTION 3

# HARD

As the heading suggests, this is the hardest section in the book. Again, we're speaking about the puzzles collectively, not individually. What is it that makes the positions more difficult? Objectively, it is mainly the length of the solution and the accompanying branches. More visualization skills are required to take the position to its appropriate depth and breadth. Subjectively, it can be anything unexpected, and if it is something unfamiliar it is also unexpected.

Additionally, there are often multiple themes, not just the one given in the caption. Naturally, this contributes to the degree of difficulty. The granddaddy of multiple themes is the imaginative #286, which begins and ends in a fork. But of course, there are others that are not so clear-cut. So how did the authors decide on their classification? If you're expecting deep soul searching and heated debate, we have to disappoint you.

A typical discussion might be:

**BA:** "What do you make of #293, overload or fork?

**FW:** "Looks more like a fork to me."

**BA:** "But we're running short of overloads."

**FW:** "Then make it an overload."

The final three positions are culled from the realm of king and pawn endgames. Most likely they are studies, but they are sufficiently game-like to be included. As to be expected they all turn on promotion while mate figures into proceedings. Also in each, there is a critical moment when the king must step outside the square of the enemy pawn, allowing the opponent to promote.

If you've gone through the previous sections thoroughly (this means more than once), then you've no doubt accumulated sufficient experience to take on the positions in the present section. Don't let the title heading discourage you. You're up to the task.

## 201. *White to Move*
(En Prise)

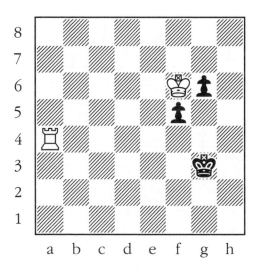

## 202. *White to Move*
(En Prise)

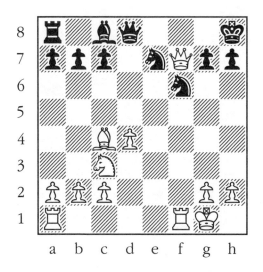

### 203. *White to Move*
(Trapping)

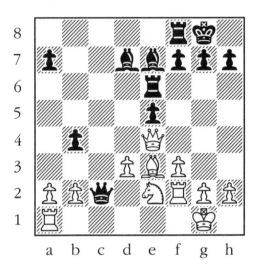

### 204. *White to Move*
(Trapping)

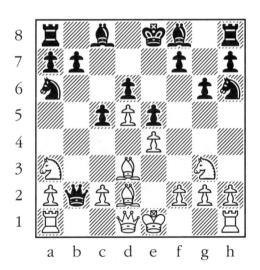

## 205. *Black to Move*
(Fork)

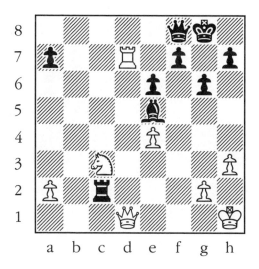

## 206. *Black to Move*
(Fork)

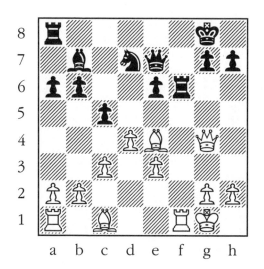

## 207. *Black to Move*
(Pin)

## 208. *White to Move*
(Pin)

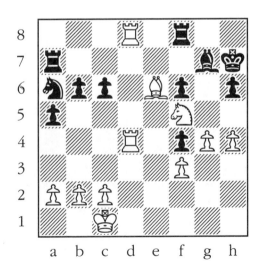

## 209. *Black to Move*
(Mating Attack)

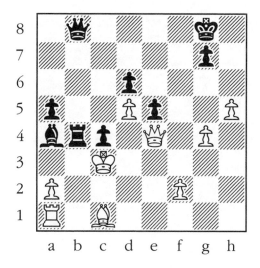

## 210. *White to Move*
(Mating Attack)

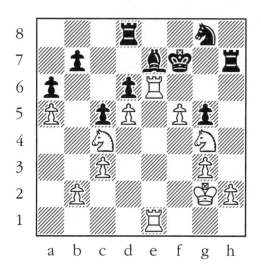

## 211. *Black to Move*
(Discovery)

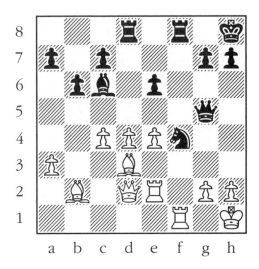

## 212. *White to Move*
(Discovery)

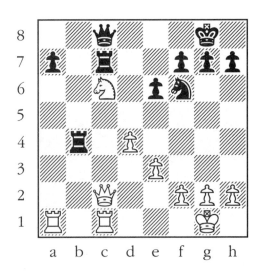

### 213. *White to Move*
(Promotion)

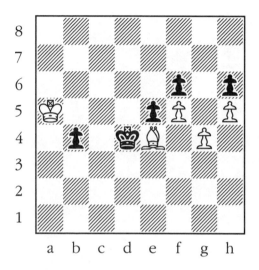

### 214. *Black to Move*
(Promotion)

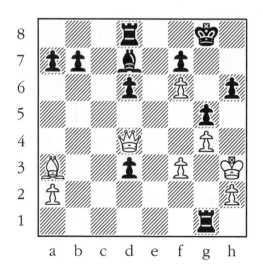

## 215. *White to Move*
(Driving Off)

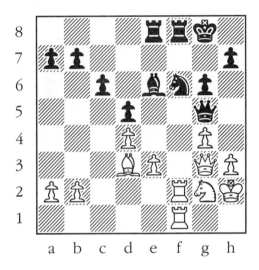

## 216. *White to Move*
(Driving Off)

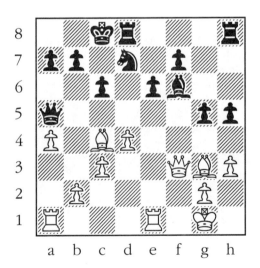

### 217. *White to Move*
(Overload)

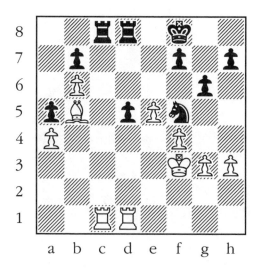

### 218. *White to Move*
(Overload)

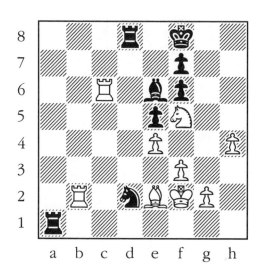

## 219. *Black to Move*
(Removing the Guard)

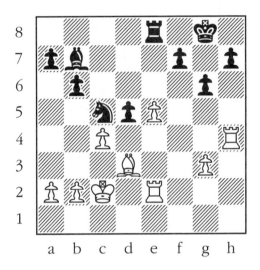

## 220. *Black to Move*
(Removing the Guard)

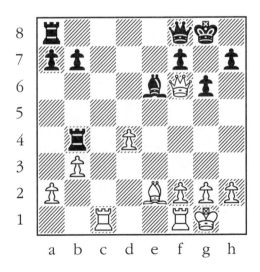

## 221. *Black to Move*
(En Prise)

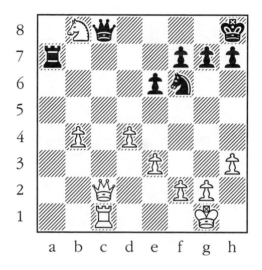

## 222. *White to Move*
(En Prise)

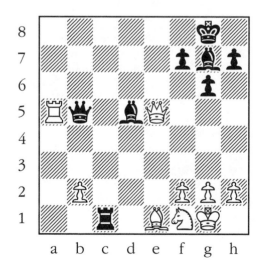

**129**

## 223. *White to Move*
(Trapping)

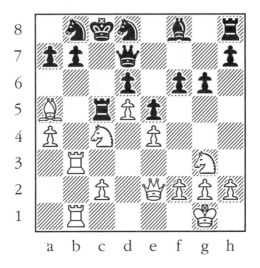

## 224. *Black to Move*
(Trapping)

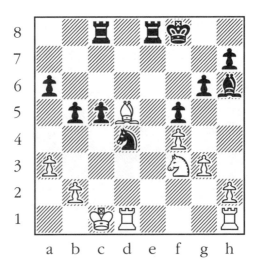

## 225. *Black to Move*
(Fork)

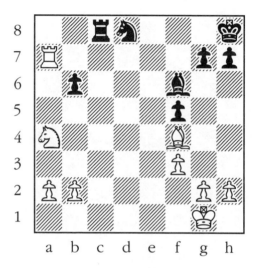

## 226. *Black to Move*
(Fork)

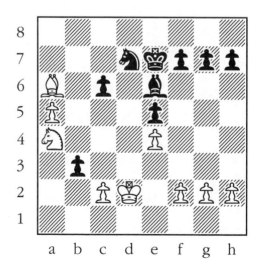

### 227. *White to Move*
(Pin)

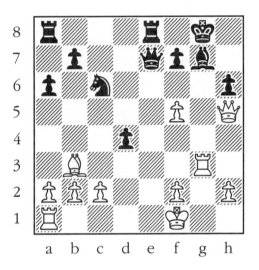

### 228. *White to Move*
(Pin)

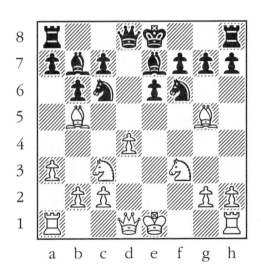

### 229. *White to Move*
(Mating Attack)

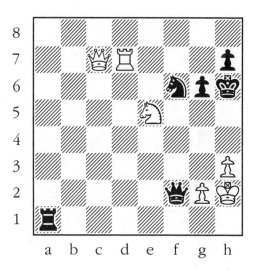

### 230. *Black to Move*
(Mating Attack)

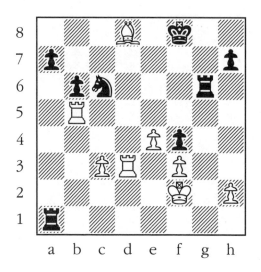

## 231. *White to Move*
(Removing the Guard)

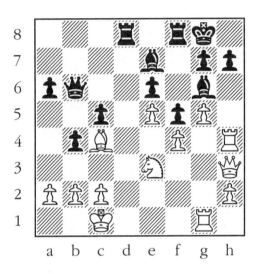

## 232. *White to Move*
(Removing the Guard)

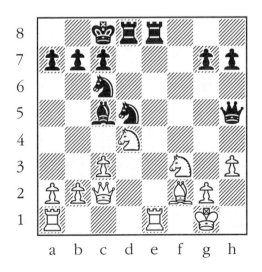

### 233. *White to Move*
(Promotion)

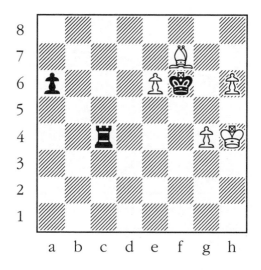

### 234. *White to Move*
(Promotion)

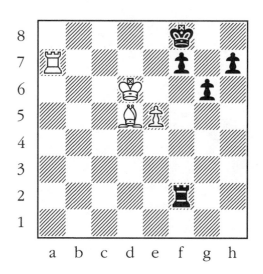

## 235. *White to Move*
(Driving Off)

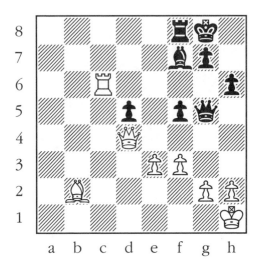

## 236. *Black to Move*
(Driving Off)

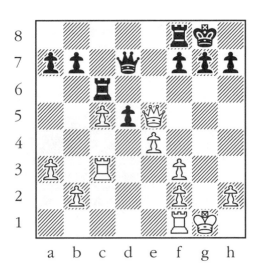

### 237. *White to Move*
(Skewer)

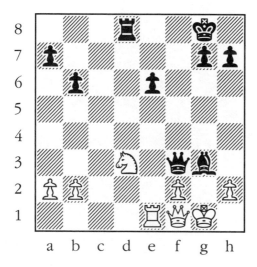

### 238. *White to Move*
(Skewer)

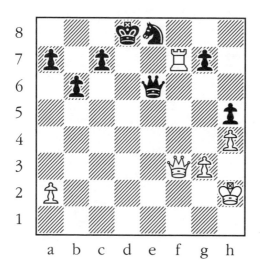

## 239. *White to Move*
(Overload)

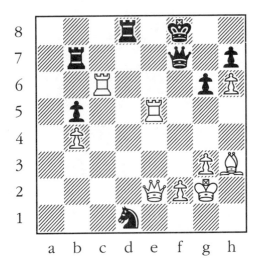

## 240. *White to Move*
(Overload)

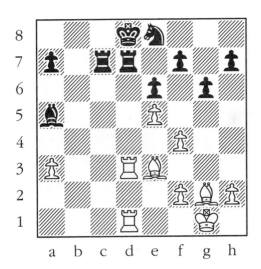

### 241. *White to Move*
(En Prise)

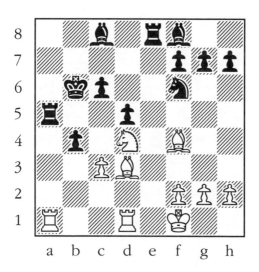

### 242. *White to Move*
(En Prise)

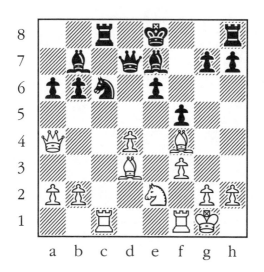

### 243. *White to Move*
(Trapping)

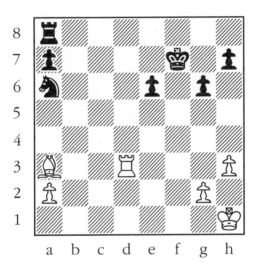

### 244. *White to Move*
(Trapping)

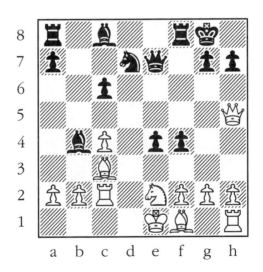

## 245. *Black to Move*
(Fork)

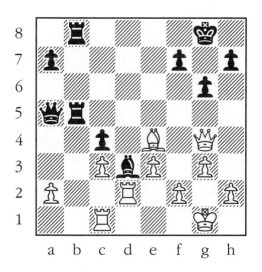

## 246. *Black to Move*
(Fork)

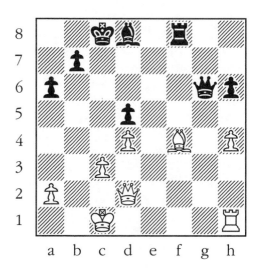

### 247. *White to Move*
(Pin)

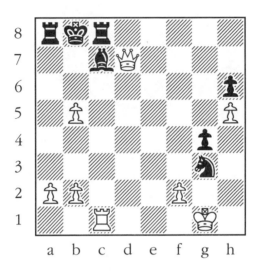

### 248. *White to Move*
(Pin)

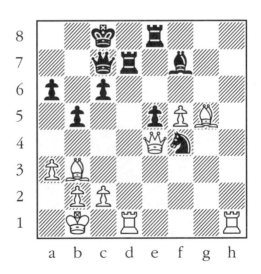

### 249. *White to Move*
(Mating Attack)

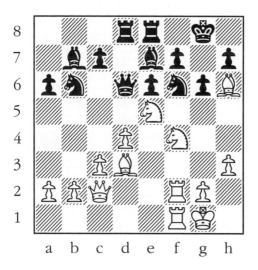

### 250. *White to Move*
(Mating Attack)

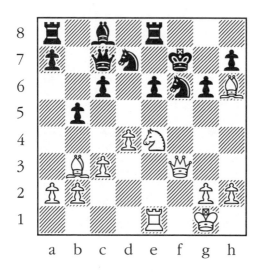

### 251. *White to Move*
(En Prise)

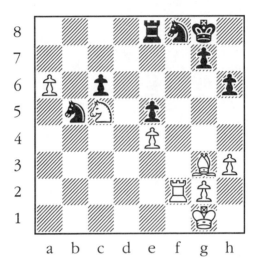

### 252. *White to Move*
(En Prise)

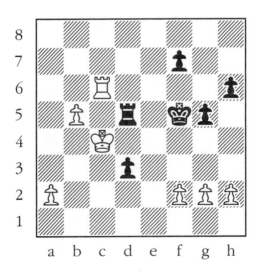

### 253. *White to Move*
(Trapping )

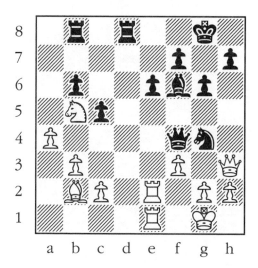

### 254. *Black to Move*
(Trapping)

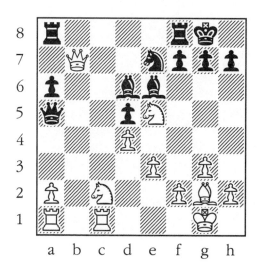

## 255. *White to Move*
(Fork)

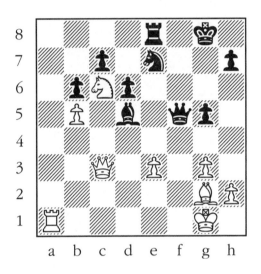

## 256. *White to Move*
(Fork)

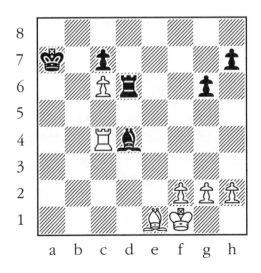

### 257. *White to Move*
(Pin)

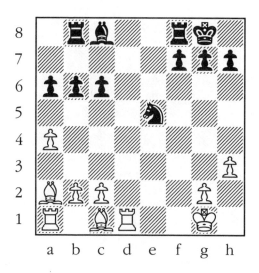

### 258. *Black to Move*
(Pin)

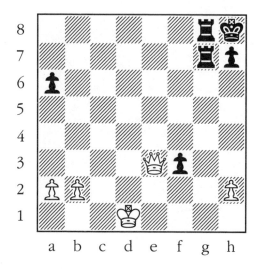

## 259. *Black to Move*
(Mating Attack)

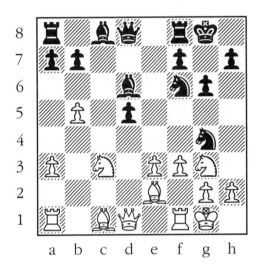

## 260. *White to Move*
(Mating Attack)

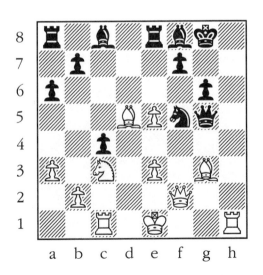

### 261. *Black to Move*
(Discovery)

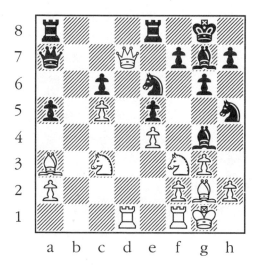

### 262. *Black to Move*
(Discovery)

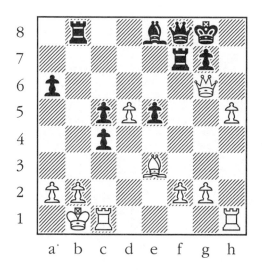

### 263. *Black to Move*
(Promotion)

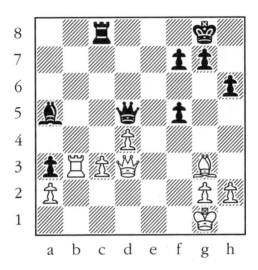

### 264. *White to Move*
(Promotion)

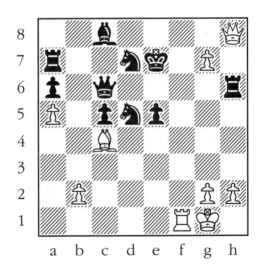

### 265. *White to Move*
(Fork)

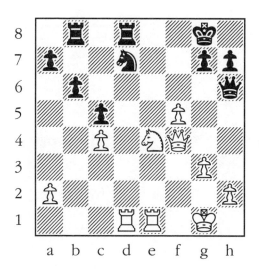

### 266. *Black to Move*
(Fork)

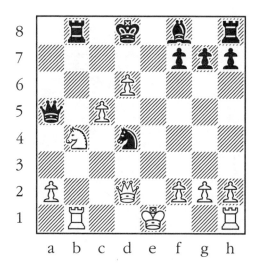

### 267. *White to Move*
(Removing the Guard)

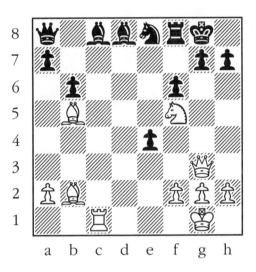

### 268. *Black to Move*
(Removing the Guard)

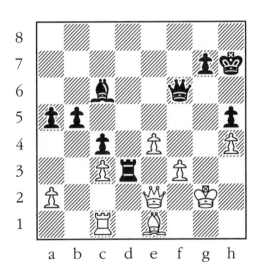

### 269. *White to Move*
(Mating Attack)

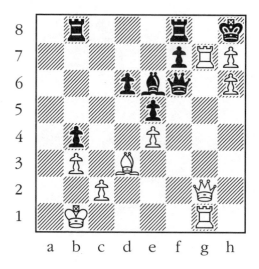

### 270. *White to Move*
(Mating Attack)

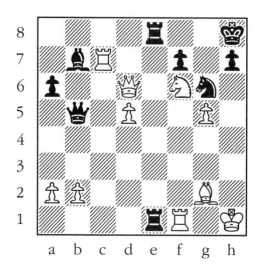

### 271. *Black to Move*
(Discovery)

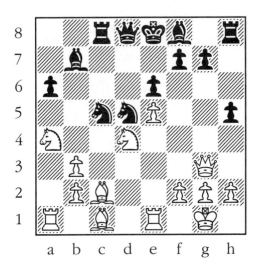

### 272. *White to Move*
(Discovery)

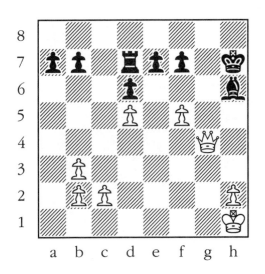

### 273. *White to Move*
(Overload)

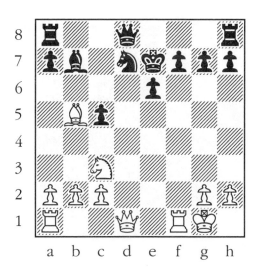

### 274. *White to Move*
(Overload)

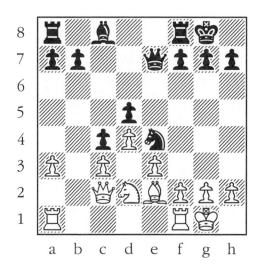

## 275. *White to Move*
(Removing the Guard)

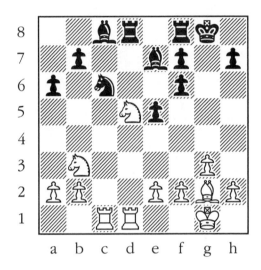

## 276. *White to Move*
(Removing the Guard)

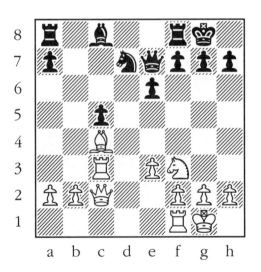

## 277. *White to Move*
(Pin)

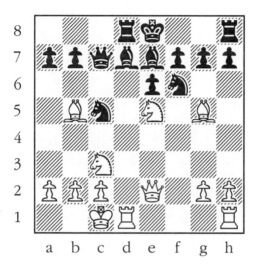

## 278. *White to Move*
(Pin)

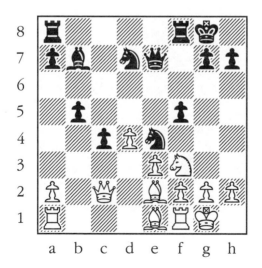

### 279. *White to Move*
(Mating Attack)

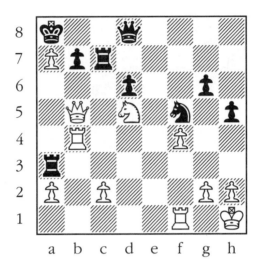

### 280. *White to Move*
(Mating Attack)

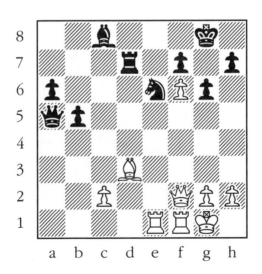

## 281. *Black to Move*
(Discovery)

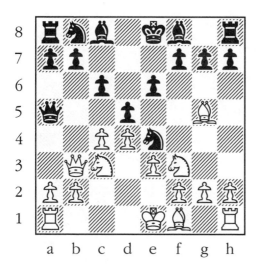

## 282. *White to Move*
(Discovery)

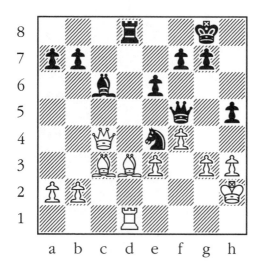

### 283. *White to Move*
(Promotion)

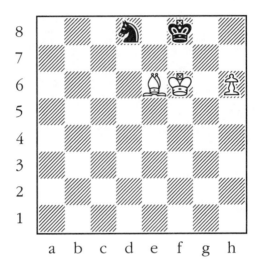

### 284. *Black to Move*
(Promotion)

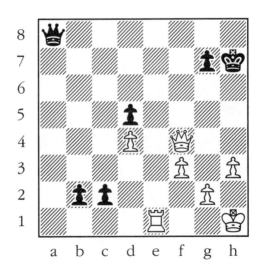

### 285. *Black to Move*
(Fork)

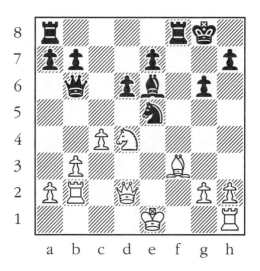

### 286. *White to Move*
(Fork)

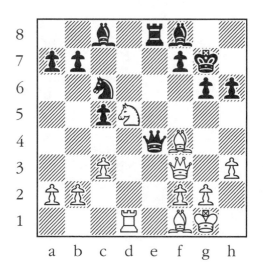

### 287. *Black to Move*
(Overload)

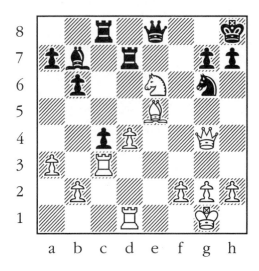

### 288. *White to Move*
(Overload)

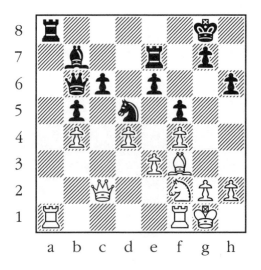

### 289. *White to Move*
(Removing the Guard)

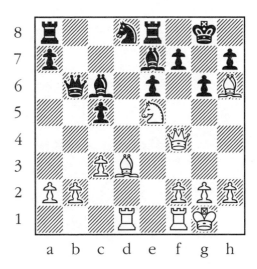

### 290. *White to Move*
(Removing the Guard)

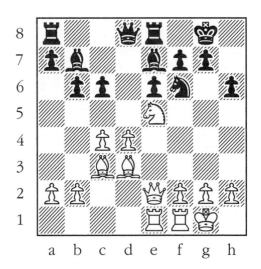

### 291. *White to Move*
(Discovery)

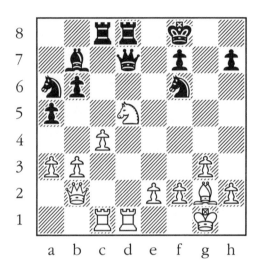

### 292. *White to Move*
(Discovery)

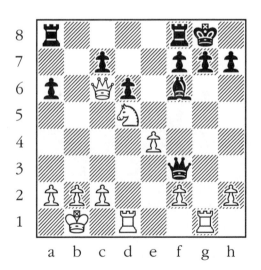

### 293. *Black to Move*
(Overload)

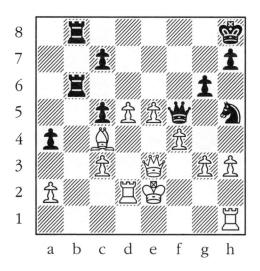

### 294. *White to Move*
(Overload)

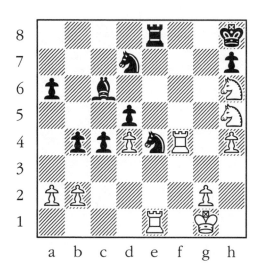

### 295. *White to Move*
(Driving Off)

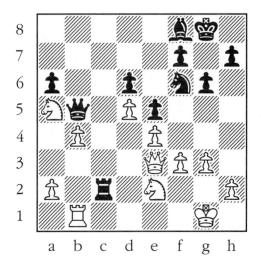

### 296. *White to Move*
(Driving Off)

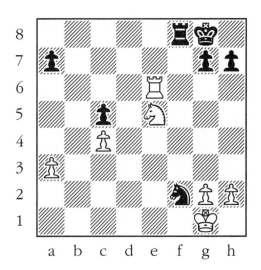

### 297. *White to Move*
(Skewer)

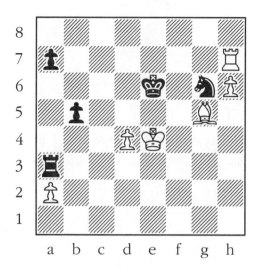

### 298. *White to Move*
(Skewer)

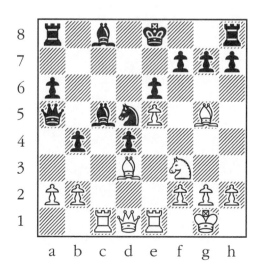

## 299. *White to Move*
(Removing the Guard)

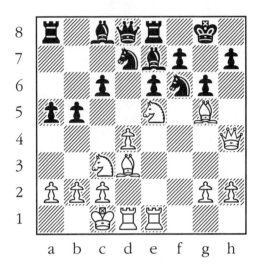

## 300. *White to Move*
(Removing the Guard)

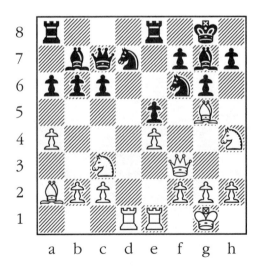

## 301. *White to Move*
(Promotion)

## 302. *White to Move*
(Promotion)

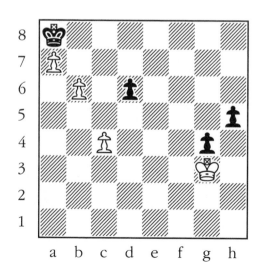

### 303. *White to Move*
(Promotion)

# SOLUTIONS

#1    From Kramnik vs. Leko, World Championship, Brissago 2004 (g#8). Taking the c1-bishop is bad; White promotes with check. Removing the a7-pawn is better, but White then takes at g5 and can put up a long resistance. Best of all is 1... h6 reserving the a7-capture for later. If 2. h4, then 2...g4, and White can resign, which is what happened.

#2    1. Nxe8 looks most convincing.

#3    The admonition is never to take the b2-pawn with the queen. Black did not heed it and now 1.Rgb1 traps the queen.

#4    The knight has strayed too far into enemy territory and now is lost after 1. Qc2.

#5    1...e5 forks bishop and knight.

#6    After 1.Nb6 White comes away with at least the exchange.

#7    1.Rh8 pins the knight and threatens 2. Nh6.

#8    Black stays afloat by 1...Bxf3 and 2...Qg5(+).

#9    1.f4 and there's nothing to be done about 2.Rg3+ For example, 1...Rf7 2. Rg3+ Kf8 3. Qd6+ Re7 4. Qd8+ Kf7 5. Qg8+ Kf6 6. Qg6#. Nor does 1...Qa2+ 2. Kh3 improve Black's situation.

#10    1.Rg3 mates at g6 unless Black gives the queen.

#11    1...Kd6 followed by 2...Ke5 and 3...Kxf6. If 2.Kc3 c5 etc.

#12    1...Qxc3 and everything hangs.

#13    Of course 1...g1/Q+ is good enough. But 1...Bg1+ 2. Kxg1 f2+ 3.Kxg2 f1/Q+ insures that the new queen stays on the board.

#14    1...b1/Q 2Rxb1 Qxb1#. What about 1...bxc1/Q+? Nothing wrong with it but the text is faster.

#15    1 Rb3 Qxc2 2. Qxe5. The mate at g7 precludes 2...Qxb3.

#16    1. Bc7 gains the exchange; if the rook moves, then Rxb7.

#17    1. Bxa6 Bxa6 2.Nc6 wins the exchange.

#18    Simplest is 1. Nxd5 Qxd5 2. Rxb6+ Also 1. Qc5 should win, and there are likely other, slower ways.

#19    1...Nc5? 2. Ne1 and White holds on to his d3 pawn. First 1...Bb4 (preventing Ne1) and then 2...Nc5 decides.

#20    1. Nxf7 Kxf7 2. Qxe6+ and Black is busted. Try 2...Kg6 3. Bd3+ Kh5 4. Qf5+ g5 5. Bxg5 hxg5 6. Qh3#.

#21    1. axb5 takes the more valuable piece.

#22    1. Bxc6 followed by BxR coming out a pawn ahead.

#23    1...g5 gets the queen.

#24    1. c4 with Nxa2 wins the bishop.

#25    No Black piece is safe: 1. Qxf6+ Kxf6 2. Ne4+ and 3. Nxc5.

#26    1. Rxf6 Kxf6 2. Be7+ and 3. Bxd8.

#27    1. Ba4 and 2. Bxc6 wins a piece.

#28    1. g4 wins the f5-knight. If it moves, then 2. Qh7# 1. Bxd4 Rxd4 2. Qxf5 also works.

#29    1. Bh6 f6 (else Qg7#) 2. Bxf8 wins the exchange.

#30    1. Rxg6 Qa1+ (1...Qxg6 2. Bf5; 1...fxg6 2. Rd7) 2. Qg1 wins.

#31    1...Nxc3 2. Q(P)xc3 dxc4.

#32    1. Ng5 and the f7-pawn is indefensible.

#33    White should avoid 1. Rxf8+ Kxf8 2. Re8+ Kg7 3. g3 h5 4. Bf5 Rc5. 1. Rc8 chases the rook from c7 and eliminates any back row funny business. If 1...Rc3 or Rb7 simply 2. Ree8 decides.

#34    1. b6 Qxd5 2. b7 and Black will have to give both queen and rook to stop White from making a new queen.

#35    1...Rb8 2. Qa4 Nxc5.

#36    Push the king away 1. Rc6+ Kd7 and you've got a piece, 2. Rxc5.

#37    1. Rh6 and there's no defense against Rh8+.

#38    1...Rd7 wins a rook or else mates. Another way is 1...Re2 2. Rg1 Re1.

#39    1. Bd5 wins a pawn, taking twice at c6, or once at c6 and e5.

#40    1. Qxd8 Qxd8 2. Rxg8 wins a piece.

#41    The queen is takeable 1... Nxc5, provided you see that 2. Rf8 is handled by 2...Rh6.

**#42** 1...Nxf7 2. Bxa8 Qxd4 preserves roughly even chances. Any other capture on f7 puts Black in a hole.

**#43** 1. b4 along with 2. Kd3 and 3. Kc4 ensnares the rook. And 1...f5 2. Kd3 changes nothing.

**#44** 1. g4 Nd6 2. Nd4 nabs the exchange.

**#45** The fork trick 1. Bh6+ Kxh6 2. Nf7+ enables White to enter. Naturally Black declines the bishop, 1...Kg8 but then 2. Nxg6 breaks through, 2...hxg6 3. Qxg6+ with mate on g7. And if 2...Bf6 3. Ne5+ etc.

**#46** 1. Qxf8+ Bxf8 2. Nf6+ and 3. Nxd7 wins the exchange.

**#47** 1...Bh3 2. Qf1 Rg6 piles up and wins the bishop. If 3. c5 then simply 3...Bxg2.

**#48** 1. Qxc8+ Bxc8 2. Bb3 recovers the queen with interest.

**#49** 1...Rgxg2 2. Rxg2 Re1+ forces 3. Qg1 losing the queen.

**#50** 1...Re8 takes away the escape squares on the e-file, setting up for 2...Bc2#.

**#51** Not 1...Qxd7? 2. Nb6. But 1...Nxd7 is OK and if 2. Rxe6 then 2...Bxd4 keeps things under control, at least for the moment.

**#52** 1...c5 blocks out the rook, leaving f4 indefensible.

**#53** 1. Bc7 c1/Q 2. Bxf4+ eliminates Black's queen after which White goes on to queen his a-pawn.

**#54** 1...Re5+ 2. Kd6 Bg6 followed by the advance of the g-pawn. If White takes, the e-pawn promotes.

**#55** 1. Nf5+ exf5 2. Rhe1 garners the queen.

**#56** 1. Rf2 followed by 2. Rf7+ is decisive.

**#57** 1. Bxe6 Qxe6 (1...Nxe6 2. Qxb6) 2. Qxc5+.

**#58** 1...Rxf5 and if 2. Nxf5 Kxe6.

**#59** 1. Bxf6 Bxf6 2. Qh7#.

**#60** 1...Rxd1 2. Rfxd1 Rxb3 gains two pieces for a rook.

**#61** 1. Rg3 wins one of the pawns at a7 or g7. If 1...Ne4 2. Qf5+ wins.

**#62** 1...Bxf2+ 2. Kxf2 Rxa1 wins the exchange and a pawn.

**#63** Black was counting on 1. Rxa4? b5 to hold his knight, but after 1. Qb3, either the knight or something else must go. Counterattack with 1...Qb6 fails to the simple 2. e3, while 1...Nb6 runs into 2. Nc6.

**#64** 1. Rf1 is answered by 1...f6. So first 1. f6+ Kh7 and then 2. Rf1 catches the queen. If 1...Qxf6 2. Nf5+ does the job.

**#65** 1...Nd1 2. Rd2 Qxc3.

#66    1. Nxf6 Bxf6 2. Nxd7+ wins some goodies.

#67    1. Rb8 Rxc5 2. d7 wins the knight back and promotes.

#68    1. Rxd1 and if 1...Nxc4 2. Rd7.

#69    1.g4+ Rxg4 2. Ra5+ wins the rook.

#70    1...Nf3 2. Qf4 Re2 and mate shortly.

#71    1. Bg6 with threats at d5 and f6. If 1...Qe6, then 2. Bf5 traps the queen.

#72    1. Rg4 with threats of 2. Rf8+ and 2. Bxe5+ decides.

#73    1. Bd7 with 2. c7 and 3. c8/Q.

#74    1. Rb3 cxb3 2. b8/Q Ke7 3. Qe5+ and 4. Qxb2.

#75    1. Rc6 drives the knight from its defense of c8. If 1...Ne8 2. Rc8 pins and wins.

#76    1. Nb4 Rcc8? 2. Bxd6. If 1... Bxg3? 2. Nxc6 Best is 1...cxb4 2. Rxc6 Nxc6 3. Bxd6 when the net effect is simplification into an ending where White is already a pawn ahead.

#77    1...Rxd4 and if 2. cxd4 Rxc1+.

#78    1. Ne4 Nxe4 (if 1...Qe7 2. Nxd6 wins a piece) 2. Rxd8.

#79    1. Rd8+ Kh7 (1...Re8{f8} drops a rook) 2. Qh4 mate.

#80    1...Kc7 along with 2...Bc6 and 3...Ra8 mate is hard to meet.

#81    1. c5 menaces a pawn fork at c6 while clearing the 4th rank. After 1...Nb8 2. Nd6+ wins the Black queen.

#82    Pick the right withdrawal square for the bishop and the game is over. 1. Bc3+ (stops ...Qe1+) 1...Bg6 2. Qf6 with mate on g7, unless Black decides to give up the queen.

#83    1.Nd6+ Kb8 2. Rxf7 traps the queen.

#84    1...b4 2. Nb1 (or Na2) 2...b3 wins a piece.

#85    1...Rxc3 2. Qxc3 (2. Nxc3 Nf3+) 2...Ne2+ Not quite so potent is 1...Qb7 when 2. Re3 provides sufficient defense for the moment.

#86    1. Bd6+ Kg7 2. Ne8+ and 3. Nc7 gets one of the Black rooks.

#87    1. Qh7+ Kf8 2. Rf1 gains the queen.

#88    1...Qd3 wins the queen as 2. Qxd3 Rxf2 is mate.

#89    1. Rxg8 Qxg8 2. Nc7 smothered mate.

#90    1...Bxh3 2. gxh3 Qxf3.

#91    1...Bxh2+ 2. Nxh2 Rxd3 gets queen and pawn for rook and bishop.

#92    1...Bf6 threatens 2...Bxd4 3. exd4 Rd3 and 4...Rxd4. If 2. Rd1 Rxa3 and if 2. Nf3 Rxe3.

**174**

#93    1. f8/N+ and mate shortly. E.g. 1...Kf6 2. Qe6+ Kg5 3. Qg6# Instead, 1. f8/Q? Ne3+ and White will be happy to draw.

#94    1...d3 2. exd3 Bf3! But not 2...Rd2+ 3. Rxd2 exd2 4. Bg4. Now both 3...Rd2+ and 3...e2 are threatened and if 3. Bg2 then 3...Bxh5 renews the threat of ...e2.

#95    1...Nd4 wins the exchange after 2. Qd2 Qxc5 3. Be3 etc. If 2. Qc3(c1) Nxe2+.

#96    1...g5 2. Bd2 Nxe5.

#97    1. Bh3 Q-moves 2. Bxc8.

#98    1. Nb7+ (controls c5) 1...Kf7 2. Rc6 winning bishop or knight.

#99    1...Rxd4 2. exd4 Rxb3.

#100   1. Qxf6 wins a knight thanks to the threat of 2. Re8+ and mate next move.

#101   1. Qc2 Rac8 2. Bc4 and White remains a piece ahead.

#102   1. Qxf4 gxf4 2. Nxd7 Black's queen was attacked on the previous move and his knight check at f4 changed nothing.

#103   1...Rd3 (a) 2. Re3 Ne2+ (b) 2. Qg4 f5.

#104   1. Rg4 gets the queen, though after 1...Rxf3 2. Rxg3 Rxg3 it's still a game.

#105   1. Nh6+ Kh8 2. Nxf7+ and 3. Nxd8 wins enough goodies.

#106   1. Rxf7 and if 1...Qxf7 2. Nd6+ gets the queen.

#107   1. Nxd7 Qxd7 2. b5 piles up and wins the c6-pawn.

#108   1. Qxd4 exd4 2. Rxe7.

#109   1...Rg3 2. Qxd4+ e5 when the main threat is 3...Rxh3+.

#110   Fastest is 1. Qe3+ Kh4 (1... Kxf6 2. Qf4#) 2. Rf3 with 3. Rh3#.

#111   1. Nxc6+ followed by 2. Nxd5+ and 3. Qxa5.

#112   1. Ne4 threatens queen, bishop, and mate at g7/h8. If 1...Qh6 then 2. Nxd6, while on 1...Be5 comes 2. Nxg5 Bxd4 3. Bxd4, winning a piece in both cases.

#113   1. b7+ Kc7 2. fxe6 Bc5 3. exf7 ties Black's pieces to watching the promotion squares. White brings his king up and wins.

#114   1. Rxb8 Rxb8 2. Nc6 Rxb3 (2...Rb7 3. Nd8+) 3. d7 Rd3 4. d8/Q.

#115   1. Nc3 R5d6 2. Bxc5.

#116   1. b4 Qxc4 2. Qxe5.

#117   1...Bxa4 and White has no good recapture: (a) 2. Qxa4 Qxb1+ (b) 2. Rxa4 Qxc3 (c) 2. Rxc8 Qe1# (d) 2. Qxh7+ Kf8 and White is losing a rook or being mated.

#118   1...Nxc4 (threat 2...Nxe3) (a) 2. Qxc4 Qxf2+ (b) 2. dxc4 Rd2 wins the queen or mates after ...Qxf2+.

#119 1. dxc5, 2. Bxf6, and 3. Qxe4 wins a pawn.

#120 If 1...e2? 2. Bc3 and White defends. So, 1...Rxe5 2. fxe5 e2 and promotes. Whether queen vs. rook ending wins is another question.

#121 1. Nxd5 wins a pawn, for if 1...gxh4 2. Nxe7+ gets the exchange.

#122 1. Rxe6. In view of the threats 2. Re8+ or 2. Re7, Black has to give up the exchange 1...Re5 2. dxe5.

#123 1...Kf8 2. Rxd2 g6 locks the bishop in. It can be further attacked and won by ...Kg7, ...Rh8, ...Nf8(g5).

#124 After 1. Bf7 Black must give the exchange 1...Re8 2. Bxe8 or else lose the g8-knight.

#125 1. Bc7 Qxc7 2. Bxd5+ and 3. Qxc6.

#126 1. Nxc8 Rxc8 (1...Qxc8 2. Nb6) 2. Bxd7+ and 3. Nb6 gaining the exchange.

#127 1. Rxe8+ Qxe8 2. Rd8 pins and wins the queen.

#128 1. Ne4 Be7 2. b4 wins the knight.

#129 1. Rf6, an elegant blocking move to set up the threat 2. Qe4 and 3. Qh7# Naturally 1...Nxf6 is met by 2. Bxf6 and 3. Qxh5. While 1...Kg7 (don't ask why Black should play this) runs into the neat step ladder 2. Rg6+Kh7 3.

Rg7+ Kh8 (3...Kh6 4. Rh7#) 4. Rh7+ Kg8 5. Rh8#.

#130 1...Qxf2+ 2. Kh1 Rd2 and White has to give up the queen to stop ...Qh2 mate.

#131 1...Qg7 2. fxg7 Kxg7 eliminates the f6-pawn providing escape after 3. Rh7+ Kf8 4. Rh8+ Ke7 etc.

#132 1. Nxb6 axb6 2. Bc4+ and mate next move.

#133 1. Qf6+ Qg5 2. Qxg5+ Kxg5 3. e7 and promotes. The bishop is pinned and may not play to g6 or d7.

#134 1. Rc8 Kxc8 2. f8/Q+ Kd7 3. Qf7+ and 4. Qc4 insures that only White gets a queen. And 4...c1/Q 5. Qxc1 doesn't count.

#135 It's a free pawn after 1. Nd5 Qd6 2. Qxc4.

#136 1. Na8 Qd8 2. Nxc6. If 1...Qa7 (a5) 2. Ra1 and 3. Reb1 traps the queen.

#137 1. Nxe5 Qd4+ 2. Kh1 Qxe5 3. Bf4 skewering queen and rook.

#138 1. Rh3 Qb4 2. Bxf6 wins a piece (2...Bxf6 3. Qxh7#).

#139 1. Bxg6 wins a pawn as 1...fxg6 is met by 2. Qh8+ and 3. Rf3+.

#140 1. Nxc6 bxc6 2. Bxe7 winning an exchange.

**176**

**#141** 1...Qc7+ (to stop Rd8+) and then 2...axb6.

**#142** Not 1...bxa6? 2. Bxa6#. But 1...Bxc5 2. dxc5 e5 winning a piece. 3...bxa6 is real threat, and so is 3...exf4+. 1...Nxc5 may also work but it's messier after 2. Qxa7.

**#143** 1. Rh3 Qg5 2. Rh5 forces Black to give up a piece: 2...Qxg2+ 3. Qxg2 Bxg2 4. Kxg2.

**#144** 1. axb5 wins a couple of pawns, or else a piece after 1...axb5 2. d5. Nor is 1...Rxb5 much use after 2. Ba4 Rb6 3. Nc4.

**#145** Nf4 Qe4 2. Qxe2 Qxe2 3. Nxe2 puts White a piece up. Less convincing is 1. Bxg7 Qe4 (a preemptive strike) 2. Qxe4 Rxe4 when Black has rook and pawn for two pieces.

**#146** 1. Rb8 Rxa2 2. Rxf8+ Kxf8 3. Bd6+ and 4. Bxc5. As for 1...Rxb8 2. Bxb8, it's just a won ending for White who has two extra pawns. Nor does 1...Nd3+ 2. Kd2 change the evaluation.

**#147** 1. Bxg6 Qxg6 2. Rg3.

**#148** 1...Qd6 leaves the c2-knight in a quandary. If 2. Rb2 Bf5 and on 2. Qb2 comes 2...Qc7 piling on.

**#149** 1. Re8 Rg8 2. Qe6 and mate next move.

**#150** After 1...Qh4 Black breaks in at h2 or g2: 2. h3 (2. Nf3 Bxf3) 2...Qg3 3. Nf3 Bxf3 4. Rxf3 and now 4...Qh2+ 5...Qh1+ and 6...Qxg2+.

**#151** 1...Nxd4 2. cxd4 Qxb5.

**#152** 1. Bd5+ discovers on the queen (1...Kf8) and picks up the bishop at a2.

**#153** 1...Rc6 2. Qxc6 Qxc6 3. Rxc6 d1/Q+. And if 2. Qe1 Rxc1 3. Qxc1 Qd1+ does the job.

**#154** First stop Black from promoting; then the rest takes care of itself:1. Rd1 Rxd1 2. Nf7+ Kg7 3. h8/Q+ Kxg6 4. Qf6+ Kh7 (4...Kh5 5. Qg5#) 5. Ng5+ Kg8 6. Qf7+ Kh8 7. Qh7#.

**#155** 1. Bg6 Qd8 2. Nf7 wins an exchange.

**#156** 1. Bxd6 Qxd6 2. Rf7+ wins the queen.

**#157** 1. Rxg8 Rxg8 2. Qxb7 mate.

**#158** 1. Nxf7+ wins the queen: 1... Rxf7 2. Qxd8+ Also 1. Qxd8 Rxd8 2. Nxf7+ and 3. Nxd8 is not bad.

**#159** 1. Rxf6 Rxf6 2. Qg5+ Kf7 and 3. Qxd5+. It's tough playing without a queen.

**#160** 1. Rxd7 Qxf4 2. Rxd8+ Rxd8 3. gxf4 wins a knight.

**#161** 1...Bh2 2. g4 Bd6 and the a3-pawn drops.

#162 After taking the loose pawn, 1. Rxc7 Black has no effective means of stopping 2. Bxe5+ Rxe5 3. Rf8 mate.

#163 1...Rd7 leaves the White knight no way out. If 2. a5, then 2...Na6. And 2. Rc1 is useless because of the back rank mate threat.

#164 1. Nb6 Ra7 2. Bb8 snares the rook.

#165 1. Be4 (a) 1...Qb5 2. Qd7 Qxe2 3. Qxb7 wins a piece. (b) 1...Qxd1 2. Rfxd1 and Black is unable to meet the dual threats 3. Bxc6 and 3. Rd7.

#166 After 1...Kd7 2. Nxa8 Qa5+ 3. Bd2 Qxa8, Black is in pretty good shape, since he has two pieces for a rook, and soon picks up the d6-pawn. For example, 4. Bf4 e5 5. Bg5 Bxd6.

#167 1. Rb2 defends the mate threat: 1...fxg2? 2. Rxg2. In view of White's far advanced b-pawn Black should head for the draw: 1...Qe1+ 2. Kh2 Qh4+ 3. Kg1 etc. But not 3. Bh3? Qf4+ with 4...Qc1+ and 5... Qxb2.

#168 1. Nxh5 picks off a loose pawn: 1...Nxh5 2. Qxh5+.

#169 1...Rh1+ 2. Kxh1 Qxf2 with 3...Rh8+ is kaput.

#170 1. Rdd7 Bxd7 2. Qxd7 with inevitable mate on h7. White can also start with 1. Qd7, but why rub it in? Plus if you're wrong...

#171 1. f5 Bh7 2. Bxd6.

#172 1. Nf5+ exf5 2. Bxc3 wins the exchange: 2...Nxc3 is illegal.

#173 1. Bxc6 Bxc6 2. Qd4 wins the knight or mates at g7.

#174 1. Nxf6 Nxf6 2. Rxf6 wins a piece. Black can't afford 2...Qxf6 3. Qh7#.

#175 1...g5 2. fxg6 Nf3+ 3. Rxf3 Rxf3 wins the exchange.

#176 1. Rb4+ Ke5 2. Rb5+ Rxb5 3. a8/Q. The queen will beat the rook but it takes a while.

#177 1. Qg4+ Kh8 2. Qg5 ganging up on f6 is decisive.

#178 1...Bg7 saves the king. Now on 2. Qd4, to save the knight, Black has 2...Bf5.

#179 1...Be5 so as to answer 2. Qxa5 with 2...Rh2# and 2. Nxe5 with 2...Rxd1+ 3. Bxd1 Qe1+ 4. Kh2 Qg1#.

#180 1. Rf7 Qg5 2. Rh7+ Kg8 3. Qf7#.

#181 1. Rxe7 Qxe7 2. Bf8+.

#182 1. Qxc7 Qxc7 2. e6+ and 3. e8/Q.

#183 With the bishop tied to the b-pawn 1. Kh6 threatens to trade queens and promote the f-pawn. For example, 1... Kf7 2. Qxe8+ Kxe8 3. Kg7 followed by 4. f7 and 5. f8/Q.

#184 1...Rxd1 2. Qxd1 Re8 3. Qg4 Re1 and the d-pawn promotes.

#185   1. Qg5 threatens both Rxd8 and Nf6+. If 1...Nd7 2. Rxd7 with the same two threats.

#186   1. Qa4 a5 2. Qc6 picks up at least a pawn.

#187   1. Ne4 piles up on the pinned f6-knight. If 1...hxg5 then 2. Nxf6+ and 3. Qh7#.

#188   1. Nxe7+ Qxe7 2. Nb5 recovers the knight and wins a pawn.

#189   First the queen enters, then the knight. When the g1-knight falls the mating threats begin in earnest. 1...Qc1+ 2. Kg2 Nf4+ 3. Kh1 (3. Kh2 Ne2+) 3...Nxh3 4. Kg2 Qxg1+ 5. Kxh3 Qxf2 6. Kg4 Qg3+ 7. Kh5 g6#.

#190   1. Bxa6 bxa6 2. Qxa6+ Kd8 3. Ba5.

#191   1. Bxh7+ Kxh7 2. Bg5+ and 3. Bxe7. Not taking the bishop, 1...Kh8, doesn't help as 2. Bg5 still wins.

#192   1. Ng5 hxg5 2. Bxb7 and 3. Bxa8 wins the exchange.

#193   The White queen cannot be in two places at the same time as shown by 1...Rxd5 2. Qxd5 Qe1+.

#194   1. Qd6 (threat 2. Qxf6+) (a) 1...Qxd6 2. Nf7# (b) 1...Rf8 2. Qxc7.

#195   After 1...Bxg5 White is unable to save both his queen and the c2-pawn.

#196   1...Rg7 2. Qe4 Rfxg3 with mate threats at g1 and h3.

#197   1. Ra1+ Kb4 2. Nc6+ Kb5 3. Nxa5.

#198   1. Bxh7+ Kxh7 2. dxe5 Q-moves 3. Rxd7.

#199   1. Bxg7 breaks in: 1...Rxg7 2. f6.

#200   1. Nxd5 wins at least a piece and probably more: (a) 1...exd5 2. Bxe7 (b) 1...Bxg5 2. Nxg5 exd5 3. Qxh7#.

#201   Not 1. Kxg6? f4, but 1. Kg5 keeps the pawns from advancing. After 1...Kf3 2. Kxg6 f4 3. Kg5 White picks up the straggler, 4. Rxf4.

#202   1. Rxf6 wins a piece: 1...gxf6 2. Qxf6# The attempt to collect the rook with the queen, 1...Qxd4+ 2. Kh1 Qxf6 leaves the back rank fatally weak, 3. Qe8+ Qf8 4. Qxf8+ Ng8 5. Qxg8#.

#203   1. Nc3, when the best Black can do is get rook and knight for his queen.

#204   1. Nc4 Qb5 (1...Qd4 2. Ne2) 2. Nxd6+ and 3. Bxb5 catches the queen.

#205   1...Rf2 gets Black out of his dilemma since 2. Rd8 runs into 2...Rf1+ and if 2. Kg1 then 2...Qc5 is sufficient.

#206   1...Rxf1+ 2. Kxf1 Nf6 wins a bishop. If White gives the queen, 3. Bxb7 Nxg4 4. Bxa8, then 4...Qf8+ 5. Bf3 Nxh2+ etc.

**179**

#207    1...Bc2 2. Rxc2 Qb1+ and 3...
Qxc2.

#208    1. R4d7 Rxd7 (or 1...Rxd8
2. Rxa7) 2. Rxd7 winning the
bishop.

#209    1...Rb2 threatens 2...Qb4#:
(a) 2. a3 Qb3# (b) 2. Qxc4
Rc2+ (c) 2. Kxc4 Qc7+ 3. Kd3
Qc2#.

#210    1. f6 Bf8 (1...Bxf6 2. Rf1) 2.
Ne5+ dxe5 3. Nxe5#.

#211    1...Nxd3 2. Rxf8+ Rxf8 when
the mate threat at f1 precludes
White from taking either queen
or knight.

#212    1. Ne7+ wins a rook after 1...
Kf8 2. Nxc8 Rxc2 3. Rxc2.

#213    1. Kxb4 Kxe4 2. g5 forces a
pawn through. If 2...fxg5 3. f6
or 2...hxg5 3. h6, and finally
2...Kxf5 3. gxh6.

#214    1...d2 2. Qxd2 (2. Qxg1 Ba4
and 3...d1/Q) 2...Bb5 with
3...Bf1# (unless White gives
up the queen).

#215    1. Rxf6 Rxf6 2. h4 pushes
the queen away and gains
something big.

#216    1. b4 Qf5 (if 1...g4 2. Qe4 and
on 1...Qb6 2. a5) 2. Qxc6+
bxc6 3. Ba6#.

#217    1. Rxd5 wins a pawn.
Whichever Black rook takes,
White takes the other.

#218    1. Rd6 wins the knight, for if
1...Rxd6 2. Rb8+ gives a back
rank mate.

#219    1...Nxd3 2. Kxd3 dxc4+ with
two pawns for the exchange. If
3. R(K)xc4 then 3...Ba6(+).

#220    1...Qd8 equalizes as White is
unable to hang on to his extra
pawn. If 2. Qxd8 (2. Qf3 Qxd4)
2...Rxd8 3. Bf3 Rdxd4.

#221    It's safe to take 1...Qxb8 as
2. Qc8+ Qxc8 3. Rxc8+ Ng8
defends, leaving Black up a
piece.

#222    Black has more loose pieces
than White: 1. Qxg7+ Kxg7 2.
Rxb5 Rxe1 (2...Bc4 3. Re5) 3.
Rxd5 wins a piece.

#223    1. Bb6 wins the exchange as
1...axb6? 2. Nxb6+ forks king
and queen.

#224    1...Red8 puts both bishop and
knight in danger. If 2. Nxd4
cxd4+. And 2. Bb7 Rc7 3. Bxa6
Ra8 wins the trapped bishop.

#225    1... b5 wins the knight for if 2.
Nc3 Bd4+ and 3...Bxa7.

#226    1...Nc5 wins a piece for if 2.
Nxc5 b2 and makes a queen.

#227    1. Qg6 Qe2+ 2. Kg1 Qe5
3. f6 piles up on the pinned
bishop and wins it. Had White
mistakenly played 1. Qxh6
instead, Black could now bail
out with 3...Qxg3+ and 4...
Bxh6.

#228    1. Ne5 Qd6 2. Qf3 wins the
pinned c6-knight. 2...Nd5 only
compounds the problem as 3.
Ne4 wins the queen or mates.

**#229**  1. Rxh7+ Nxh7 2. Ng4+ and 3. Nxf2 If 1...Kg5 2. Nf7+ Kf5 3. Qe5#.

**#230**  1...Rag1 prepares a mate with 2...R6g2. After 2. Rf5+ Ke8 3. Rxf4, it's still a mate with 3...R6g2+ 4. Ke3 Re1# So White has to give up a piece by 3. Bg5 Rxg5.

**#231**  1. Rxh7 Bxh7 2. g6 Bxg6 3. Rxg6. First e6 falls, then f5, and Black's whole position crumbles.

**#232**  1. Nxc6 Bxf2+ 2. Qxf2 bxc6 3. Qxa7.

**#233**  1. e7 Kxf7 2. e8/Q+ Kxe8 3. h7 and queens. The king interferes with the rook which cannot guard h8 from c8. If 1...Kxe7 2. h7 Rc8 3. Bg8, blocking the rook out.

**#234**  White clears a path for the pawn after which his king provides an escort: 1. Rxf7+ Rxf7 2. Bxf7 Kxf7 3. Kd7 etc.

**#235**  1. h4 tickles the queen which must retain her guard over g7. But after 1...Qg3 2. Rxh6 wins a pawn as 2...gxh6 3. Qh8 is mate.

**#236**  White defends on 1...Rg6+ 2. Kh1 Qh3 3. Rg1: also after 1...Qh3 2.f4 Rg6+ 3. Rg3. This second line of defense can be knocked out by 1...d4 pushing the rook to an undefended square, 2. Rd3; then follows 2...Qh3 and 3...Rg6+ winning the queen or mating.

**#237**  1. Re3 Bxf2+ 2. Qxf2 Qd1+ 3. Ne1 and White keeps his extra piece.

**#238**  1. Qa8+ Qc8 2. Qd5+ Nd6 3. Rf8+ and 4. Rxc8.

**#239**  Black's rook can't keep track of both his knight and his back rank. So 1. Qxd1 Rxd1 2. Rc8+ and Black must return the queen with interest.

**#240**  White can zap the a7-pawn after taking twice on d7, but there's more to be had. 1. Bc6 Rxd3 (1...Rxc6 2. Rxd7+) 2. Rxd3+ Ke7 3. Bc5+ Nd6 4. exd6+.

**#241**  The rook is loose, 1. Rxa5. For if 1...Kxa5 2. Bc7+ Ka4 and 3. Ra1 is mate.

**#242**  The a6-pawn can be captured, 1. Bxa6, as the pinning 1...Ra8 is met by 2. Bxb7 Rxa4 3.Bxc6.

**#243**  1. Rd6 Nb8 2. Rd8 followed by 3. Bd6 and 4. Rxb8 wins a piece.

**#244**  1...Ne5 threatens mainly 2...Bg4 but also 2...Nd3+. After 2. Bxb4 Nd3+ 3. Kd1 Qxb4 4. Nc3 White's position is creaking. Black can already lift a pawn with 4...Qxc4 or 4...Nxb2+.

**#245**  Black wins the bishop after 1...f5 2. Bxf5 Rxf5.

**#246**  1...Qe4 forks rook and bishop. The only defense 2. Rf1, stumbles into a pin and then 2...Bc7 is decisive.

*#247* Not 1. fxg3? Bb6+ and ... Rxc1, but first 1. Rc6 and if 1...Ne2+ Kf1 Nf4 then 3. b6 wins E.g. 3...Rxa2 bxc7+ Kb7 5. Rc1 etc.

*#248* 1. Bxf7 (a) 1...Rxf7 2. Bxf4 and the e-pawn is pinned. (b) 1...Rxd1+ 2. Rxd1 Qxf7 3. Qxc6+ Kb8 4. Rd7.

*#249* White smashes through with 1. Nxf7 Kxf7 2. Bxg6+ Kg8 (2...hxg6 3. Qxg6#) 3. Bxh7+ Kh8 (3...Nxh7 4. Qg6+ and 5. Qg7#) 4. Ng6+ Kxh7 5. Nf8+ Kh8 (5...Kxh6 6. Qg6#) 6. Rxf6 Rxf8 (else Qh7#) 7. Rf7, after which Qh7# is inevitable.

*#250* 1. Ng5+ Kg8 (1...Ke7 2. Rxe6+ Kd8 3. Nf7#) 2. Rxe6 Rxe6 3. Bxe6+ Kh8 4. Nf7+ Kg8 5. Ne5+ Kh8 6. Nxd7 and wins. E.g. 6...Nxd7 7. Qf7; 6...Qxd7 7. Qxf6+ or 6...Qd8 7. Bg5.

*#251* The e-pawn is takeable: 1. Bxe5 Rxe5 2. Rxf8+ Kxf8 3. Nd7+ and 4. Nxe5.

*#252* 1. Kxd5 d2 2. g4+ Kxg4 3. Rc4+ and 4. Rd4 stops the pawn.

*#253* 1. Qxg4 Qxg4 2. fxg4 Bxb2 3. c3 traps the bishop. After 3... Bxc3 4. Nxc3 White should win the endgame.

*#254* 1...Rab8 (a) 2. Qa7 Nc8 3. Nc6 Qa4 (b) 2. Nc6 Nxc6 3. Qxc6 Rb6. In both cases Black catches the queen.

*#255* 1. e4 Bxe4 2. Bxe4 Qxe4 3. Re1 and takes at e7. The fork sets up the skewer.

*#256* 1. Bb4 Rd5 2. Rxd4 Rxd4 3. Bc5+ and 4. Bxd4.

*#257* 1. Bf4 wins the exchange. 1...f6 is illegal and 1...Re8 2. Bxe5 Rxe5 Rd8+ is a back rank mate. So, 1...Nd7 2. Bxb8 Nxb8.

*#258* 1...f2 2. Qxf2 Rg1+ 3. Ke2 Rg2. If 2. Ke2, then 2...Rf8 3. Kf1 Rg1+.

*#259* 1...Nxh2 2. Kxh2 Ng4+ 3. fxg4 Qh4+ 4. Kg1 Bxg3 and mate shortly.

*#260* 1. Ne4 Qxe3+ (what else?) 2. Qxe3 Nxe3 3. Nf6+ Kg7 4. Rh7#.

*#261* 1...Qxd7 2. Rxd7 Nd4 wins material in view of the threats 3...Nxf3+ and 3...Bxd7.

*#262* 1...Rxb2+ 2. Kxb2 Rxf2+ and 3...Bxg6. Even stronger is 1... Rxf2 2. Qe6+ Bf7 winning the queen or mating.

*#263* 1...Qxb3 2. axb3 a2 3. Qd1 Bxc3 and 4...a1/Q.

*#264* 1. Rf7+ Kxf7 (1...Kd6 2. Qxh6+ or 1...Ke6 2. Qxh6+ Kxf7 3. Qc6) 2. g8/Q+ Ke7 3. Qd8+ with 4. Qxh6+ wraps things up nicely.

*#265* 1. Qxh6 gxh6 2. Rxd7 Rxd7 3. Nf6+ and 4. Nxd7.

*#266* 1...Rxb4 2. Rxb4 Qxb4 3. Qxb4 Nc2+ and 4...Nxb4.

**#267** 1. Bc6 Bb7 2. Bxe8 Rxe8 3. Qxg7 mate.

**#268** 1...Qf4 2. Rd1 Rxf3 3. Qxf3 Bxe4 gains the queen.

**#269** The trick is to get rid of the h-pawns, opening the h-file to get at Black's king. It's done by 1. Rg8+ Kxh7 2. Rg7+ Kh8 3. h7 with 4. Rg8+ Kxh7 5. Rh1+.

**#270** 1. Rxf7 Rxf1+ 2. Kh2 Re7 (2...Rxf6 3. Qxf6+ and mate next) 3. Qd8+ (or 3. Qxe7, but at the board it's easier to calculate the checks) 3...Qe8 4. Qxe8+ Rxe8 5. Rxh7#. The Arabian mating pattern with rook and knight.

**#271** 1...Nb4 2. Be3 (or 2. Nxc5 Rxc5) 2...Nxa4 and 3...Nxc2.

**#272** 1. f6 (a) 1...e6 2. dxe6 fxe6 3. Qxe6 Rc7 4. Qe7+ (b) 1...Rd8 2. fxe7 Re8 3. Qd7 (c) 1...Rc7 2. Qe4+ and 3. fxe7.

**#273** 1. Bxd7 is an extra piece for White as 1...Qxd7 2. Rxf7+ drops the house.

**#274** 1. Nxe4 Qxe4 2. Qxe4 dxe4 3. Bxc4. If 1...Bf5 then 2. f3 (a) 2...dxe4 3. Bxc4 (b) 2...Bg6 3. Qd2 etc.

**#275** 1. Rxc6 (a) 1...bxc6 2. Nxe7+ (b) 1...Rxd5 2. Bxd5.

**#276** 1. Bb5 followed by 2. Bxd7 and 3. Rxc5 wins a pawn.

**#277** 1. Nxd7 Ncxd7 (If 1...Nfxd7 2. Bxe7 Kxe7 3. Nd5+ Nor does 2...Qf4+ 3. Kb1 change anything.) 2. Bxf6 Bxf6 (Or

2...gxf6 3. Rxd7 Rxd7 4. Rd1 Bd6 5. Bxd7+ Qxd7 6. Ne4) 3. Rxd7 Rxd7 4. Rd1 and White emerges a piece ahead after taking at d7. White could also begin with 1. Bxf6.

**#278** 1. Qb2 Bc6 (1...a6 2. Bxc4+) 2. Bb4 Nd6 3. Ne5 Rac8 4. Qa3 Rf6 5. Qxa7 wins a pawn for a start.

**#279** 1. Nb6+ Kxa7 2. Ra4+ Rxa4 3. Qxa4+ Kxb6 4. Rb1+ Kc5 5. Rb5+ Kc6 6. Ra5+ and mate next move.

**#280** White breaks in with 1. Rxe6 fxe6 2. f7+ Kf8 3. Qf6 and 4. Qh8+.

**#281** 1...Nxg5 2. Nxg5 dxc4 and 3...Qxg5 wins a piece. Less effective is 1...dxc4 2. Qa4.

**#282** There's no good discovery as yet, 1. Bxe4 being met by 1...Rxd1 2. Bxf5 Rh1#. However, 1. g4 makes an escape for the king at g3, forcing 1...Qb5, when the queens come off the board and the game levels out.

**#283** White has to stay alert: 1. h7 Nf7 2. Bxf7 is stalemate. But 1. Kg6 Nxe6 2.h7 Nf4+ 3.Kh6 works just fine.

**#284** Not 1...c1/Q? 2. Rxc1 bxc1/Q 3. Qxc1, nor 1...b1/Q 2. Qf5+ and Rxb1. 1...Qc6! sets everything up, avoiding White tricks.

**#285** 1...Bxc4 wins a pawn, since Black wins the exchange on 2. bxc4 Qxb2 3. Qxb2 Nd3+ and 4...Nxb2.

#286    White wins the exchange starting with knight fork, then a double check, followed by a skewer, and finishing with a rook fork. Here it is 1. Nf6 Kxf6 2. Be5+ Kxe5 3. Qxe4+ Kxe4 4. Re1+ Kf5 5. Rxe8 Be6 6. Rxf8. Black momentarily clips a pawn with 6...Bxa2 but 7. Rc8 with 8. Rc7 gets everything back.

#287    1...Nxe5 2. dxe5 Rxd1+ 3. Qxd1 Qxe6 takes a piece.

#288    1. Rxa8+ Bxa8 2. Bxd5 exd5 (2...cxd5 3. Qc8+) 3. Qxf5 wins a pawn in view of 3... Rxe3? 4. Qc8+.

#289    1. Bxg6 fxg6 2. Rxd8 Raxd8 3. Qf7+ and mate next move.

#290    1. Nxf7 Kxf7 2. Qxe6+ Kf8 3. Bg6 and Qf7#.

#291    There should be more than one good move here for White. Perhaps the most convincing is 1. Ne3 attacking queen, bishop and knight. After 1...Qc7 comes 2. Qxf6 Bxg2 3. Nf5.

#292    1. e5 wins the bishop for if 1... Bxe5 2. Ne7+ Kh8 3. Qxf3 wins the queen.

#293    1...Nxg3+ 2. Qxg3 Qe4+ 3. Qe3 Qxh1 picks up the exchange. 4. e6 can be dealt with by 4...Rb2 5. e7 Rxd2+ 6.Qxd2 (if 6. Kxd2 Rb2+ 7. Kd3 Qb1#) 6...Qe4+ etc.

#294    1. Rg4 (threat 2. Nf7#) (a) 1... Nd6 2. Rxe8+ Nxe8 3. Nf7# (b) 1...Rf8 2. Rg8+ Rg8 3. Nf7#.

#295    1. Nc3 Qd7 (threat 2...Qh3) 2. Rc1 Rb2 3. Rb1 Rc2 4. Rc1 with repetition of position, forcing a draw. White must avoid 2. Qd3? Qa7+ 3. Kh1 Qf2, breaking in.

#296    1. Nd7 Rd8 2. Rd6 Ne4 3. Nf6+ Nxf6 4. Rxd8+ wins exchange.

#297    1. Rg7 Nh8 2. d5+ Kd6 3. Be7+ and 4. Bxa3.

#298    1. Qc2 Be7 2. Qxc8+ Rxc8 3. Rxc8+ Kd7 4. Rxh8 with two rooks and a bishop for the queen.

#299    White lifts a piece by 1. Nxc6 Qb6 2. Nxe7+ Rxe7 3. Bxf6 Nxf6 4. Qxf6.

#300    1. Rxd7 Nxd7 (1...Qxd7 2. Bxf6) 2. Qxf7+ Kh8 3. Rd1 Rad8 4. Bxd8 Rxd8 5. Nf3 threatening 6. Ng5, 7. Qg8+ and a smothered mate. In any case White has already won a pawn and there's more to come.

#301    White gets nowhere with 1. Ke4 c5 2. Kd3 Ke8 3. Kc4 Kd7. But if the Black king stands on e8, he can take the c5-pawn. The way to get there is by 1. Kf4 c5 2. Ke4 Ke8 3. Kd3 Kd7 4. Kc4 Ke8 5. Kxc5 d3 6. Kd6 Kf7 (or 6...d2 7. Ke6 d1/Q 8. f7#) 7. Kd7 d2 8. d8/Q+ and wins. At move one, Black can stall with 1...c6, but then White can also temporize 2. Kf3, and after 2...c5 (or 2...Ke8) 3. Ke4, he arrives at the position he's aiming for.

#302  White can easily make a draw, shuttling his king back and forth between f4/h4 and g3. Black will have to likewise at a8/b7. But if White wants to win he must get his king to c7. 1. Kf4 Kb7 2. c5 dxc5 (otherwise 3. c6+) 3. Ke5 g3 (3...c4 is no better; White proceeds as in the main line) 4. Kd6 g2 5. a8/Q+ Kxa8 6. Kc7 g1/Q 7. b7+ Ka7 8. b8/Q+ Ka6 9.Qb6#.

#303  The first step is to get the White pawns to the fifth rank. 1. Ke4 Kg4 2. h4 Kh5 3. Kf4 Kh6 4. g4 Kg6 5. h5+ Kh6 6. Ke4 Kg5 7. Kf3 Kh6 8. Kf4 Kh7 9. g5 Kg7. Next is to get the pawns to the sixth rank. Here the g-pawn must precede the h-pawn. 10. g6 Kh6 11. Kg4 Kg7. Now comes the moment of truth; the king steps on to the 5th rank, allowing the d-pawn to run. 12. Kg5 d3 13. h6+ Kg8 14. Kf6 d2 15. h7+Kh8 16. Kf7 d1/Q 17. g7+ Kxh7 18. g8/Q+ Kxh6 19. Qg6#.

# TACTICS INDEX

The numbers following each tactic listed below represent the puzzle numbers in this book.

**Discovery:** 61, 62, 71, 72, 81, 82, 91, 92, 111, 112, 151, 152, 171, 172, 181, 182, 191, 192, 211, 212, 261, 262, 271, 272, 281, 282, 291, 292

**Driving Off:** 15, 16, 35, 36, 75, 76, 95, 96, 115, 116, 135, 136, 155, 156, 195, 196, 215, 216, 235, 236, 295, 296

**En Prise:** 1, 2, 11, 12, 21, 22, 31, 32, 41, 42, 51, 52, 101, 102, 121, 122, 141, 142, 161, 162, 201, 202, 221, 222, 241, 242, 251, 252

**Fork:** 5, 6, 25, 26, 45, 46, 55, 56, 65, 66, 85, 86, 105, 106, 125, 126, 145, 146, 165, 166, 175, 176, 185, 186, 205, 206, 225, 226, 245, 246, 255, 256, 265, 266, 285, 286

**Mating Attack:** 9, 10, 29, 30, 49, 50, 69, 70, 79, 80, 109, 110, 129, 130, 149, 150, 169, 170, 179, 180, 189, 190, 209, 210, 229, 230, 249, 250, 259, 260, 269, 270, 279, 280

**Overload:** 17, 18, 57, 58, 89, 90, 117, 118, 157, 158, 193, 194, 217, 218, 239, 240, 273, 274, 287, 288, 293, 294

**Pin:** 7, 8, 27, 28, 47, 48, 67, 68, 77, 78, 87, 88, 107, 108, 127, 128, 147, 148, 167, 168, 177, 178, 187, 188, 207, 208, 227, 228, 247, 248, 257, 258, 277, 278

**Promotion:** 13, 14, 33, 34, 53, 54, 73, 74, 93, 94, 113, 114, 133, 134, 153, 154, 183, 184, 213, 214, 233, 234, 263, 264, 283, 284, 301, 302, 303

**Remove Guard:** 19, 20, 39, 40, 59, 60, 99, 100, 119, 120, 131, 132, 139, 140, 159, 160, 173, 174, 199, 200, 219, 220, 231, 232, 267, 268, 275, 276, 289, 290, 299, 300

**Skewer:** 37, 38, 97, 98, 137, 138, 197, 198, 237, 238, 297, 298

**Trapping:** 3, 4, 23, 24, 43, 44, 63, 64, 83, 84, 103, 104, 123, 124, 143, 144, 163, 164, 203, 204, 223, 224, 243, 244, 253, 254

# GREAT CHESS BOOKS FROM CARDOZA PUBLISHING

**303 TRICKY CHECKMATES** by Fred Wilson and Bruce Alberston - Both a fascinating challenge and great training tool, this collection of two, three and bonus four move checkmates is great for advanced beginning, intermediate and expert players. Mates are in order of difficulty, from simple to complex positions. Learn the standard patterns and stratagems for cornering the king: corridor and support mates, attraction and deflection sacrifices, pins and annihilation, the quiet move, and the dreaded zugzwang. Examples from actual games illustrate a wide range of tactics from classics right up to the 1990's. 192 pages, $12.95.

**202 CHECKMATES FOR CHILDREN** by Fred Wilson & Bruce Alberston - Veteran chess teachers and authors, Wilson and Alberston, who specialize in teaching chess to children, present 202 fascinating puzzles that are both instructional and fun. Large diagrams and clearly explained solutions will thrill kids as they work their way through the concepts while they have fun with chess. Perfect for kids! The authors should know: They have used these puzzles in their lessons for years. Oversized. 160 pages, $9.95.

**303 TRICKY CHESS TACTICS** by Fred Wilson and Bruce Alberston - Both a fascinating challenge and great training tool, this is a fun and entertaining collection of two and three move tactical surprises for the advanced beginner, intermediate, and expert player. Tactics are arranged by difficulty so that a player may measure progress as he advances from simple to the complex positions. The examples, drawn from actual games, illustrate a wide range of chess tactics from old classics right up to the 1990's. 192 pages, $12.95.

**303 TRICKY CHESS PUZZLES** by Fred Wilson & Bruce Alberston - An entertaining and instructive collection of carefully selected tactical chess puzzles will pay immediate dividends at the board and make any reader a better player. The authors—both veteran professional chess instructors—have collected or created 303 typical game situations. Finding the right answer will bring about a forced checkmate or a winning material superiority. Divided into three chapters, each filled with 101 large, clear diagrams, this book runs the entire gamut of necessary tactical knowledge. This a perfect workbook for anyone who wants to sharpen their budding chess expertise. 192 pages, $12.95.

**10 MOST COMMON CHESS MISTAKES and How to Fix Them** by Larry Evans This fascinating collection of 218 errors, oversights, and outright blunders, not only shows the price great players pay for violating basic principles but how to avoid these mistakes in your own game. You'll be challenged to choose between two moves, the right one or the one actually played. From neglecting development, king safety, misjudging threats and premature attacks, to impulsiveness, snatching pawns, and basic inattention, you receive a complete course in where you can go wrong and how to fix it. 256 pgs, $14.95.

**ONE MOVE CHECKMATES** by Eric Schiller - This great book for beginning players covers the most basic of mates—the one move checkmate! Schiller presents different game positions where you must find the move that instantly wins the game. You'll learn how to make the final move with all the pieces—knights, bishops, rooks, pawns, queens and even the king. This great training tool is perfect if you're new to the game of chess! This fun and easy workbook is a great learning tool. Two hundred instructive and challenging mates are a perfect compliment to the chessboard! 128 pages, $9.95.